Influencing Patterns for Change:

A Human Systems Dynamics Approach for Leaders

Royce Holladay & Kristine Quade

Human Systems Dynamics Institute
Dynamical Leadership Academy

Printed in the United States of America.

ISBN is 1440415927

Words of Praise
for
Influencing Patterns for Change
A Human Systems Dynamics
Primer for Leaders

It's a ground-breaking primer to focus change leaders on the differences that make a difference! Human Systems Dynamics takes organization complexity and explains it with elegant simplicity."

Margaret Seidler
author of
Power Surge: A Conduit for Enlightened Leadership

"Influencing Patterns for Change: A Human Systems Dynamics Primer for Leaders" belongs on every 21st century leader's bookshelf. With its focus on the "sticky issues" of real work, "Influencing Patterns" offers new ways of looking at complex problems. Full of useful, practical ideas and tools, any "change leader" -- and these days, who isn't? -- will benefit from this book's simple, yet practical approach to influencing change by influencing patterns. I highly recommend it.

Larry Solow, President
3-D Change, Inc

Thank you!!! Authors Holladay and Quade have given us a simple, easy-to-use handbook for leaders to understand why our teams function the ways they do. In a military environment we react to forces we have neither physical nor emotional control of and only inferred intelligence. Our human systems must change quickly and effectively because lives depend upon fast decision making. This Primer is the perfect reference guide for understanding how and why our units are responding, and it provides leaders the ability to influence internal change quickly.

Kent Hann
Col, USA, (ret)

TABLE OF CONTENTS

Acknowledgements

We wish to acknowledge the early coaching efforts of Associates of Human Systems Dynamics Institute, Darlene Goetzman, Linda Stevenson, Anne Sturdivant and Barb Tuckner. The early framing we did with them estalbished the structure for the building blocks of this Primer. Together with them we wandered in the Unorganized Zone, migrating toward the Organized Zone with recommendations about how to frame the concepts and format. Thank you for your input.

Readers and editors provided invaluable input on readability and understandability of the Primer. The recommended improvements created clarity of focus and options we had not considered. Thank you to Patricia Denni, Dave Dudycha, Peter Freedman, Jo Klemm, Danielle Leggett, and Margaret Seidler for taking the time to make the content richer and more readable.

Glenda Eoyang provided us with encouragement, leadership and guidance all the way through this project. She was our grounding rod for both content and perspective. Through her support and teaching, Glenda lives the simple rules of HSD and demonstrates her founding principle of sharing what she knows in order to get these understandings out to the world.

We want to especially acknowledge the concrete coaching, deep questioning and different perspective of Kent Hann, who read, reacted, debated, and offered suggestions all along the way. His contributions provided significant improvements at critical junctures.

Thanks to all the Associates who have shared your stories, insights, and learning in the Human Systems Dynamics Institute Professional Certification programs. As Teaching Assistants, we have learned from you and with you. In addition, Pat Seppanen, Myron Lowe, Jim Roussin, Julia Herzing, Dee Krengel, Megan Rounds, Larry Solow, Janice Dowling, and Mary Nations cheered from the side and provided encouragement during moments of need.

Royce - I especially wish to thank Kristine for joining me in this project and for making the journey an exploration into new learning. Also thanks to Glenda for the years of patience as I learned and used and explored with you. Thanks to Leslie for her tenacious pursuit of the writer in me and to Jo for her support and cheers. Finally thanks to my daughters, Toni Martinez and Tori Chandler for always listening to my stories and for their belief in me.

Kristine - I wish especially to thank supportive friends and colleagues of the Human Systems Dynamics Institute, most specifically Glenda Eoyang for her encouragement, critical thinking and investigative approach, without which this Primer would never have been published and co-author, Royce Holladay, for her incredible grasp of the nuances of the material, willingness to do the hard work, and ever-supportive nature. My sincerest thanks go to my husband for his love, support, and most of all for holding me together during times when I felt stretched and overwhelmed. Thanks to the whole "Primer" team for hanging in there and making this possible!

Royce Holladay is a consultant, writer, poet, and artist. She is also a change agent who is committed to bringing about organizational and societal change by focusing on how groups can build their adaptive capacities to address issues of justice, diversity and inclusion, peace, and personal fulfillment of individuals.

Working in complexity and Social Sciences. As one of the founding members and the Director of The Network for the Human Systems Dynamics Institute, Royce has worked with Executive Director, Glenda Eoyang, to expand the field of HSD and to support the growing network of Associates who have participated in the certification program offered by HSD Institute. For more information about Human Systems Dynamics Institute, please visit their website at www.hsdinstitute.org.

Royce is an engaging and skilled speaker, teacher and facilitator, and has presented at national and international conferences for Organization Development Network, American Association for School Administrators, American Society for Training and Development, and the American Evaluation and Research Association, as well at for state and regional conferences in Texas, North Carolina, Washington, Louisiana, and Minnesota.

A prolific writer, Royce uses language, images, and physical engagement to convey complex ideas in simple, applicable terms. Her publications include *HSD@Work: Frequently Asked Questions about Human Systems Dynamics,* and *Legacy: Sustainability in Complex Adaptive Systems.* She was a contributing author in *Voices From the Field: An Introduction to Human Systems Dynamics.* She is also currently working on a book of poetry, *Women In My Life*, due to be published in early 2009.

Royce can be contacted at rholladay@hsdinstitute.org.

Kristine Quade has integrated a highly effective Organization Development approach combining small and large group techniques with a proven international success record. As an independent consultant, she brings years of experience in guiding teams, drawing from divergent areas within organizations and across boundaries of high-impact issues. Kristine has facilitated leadership alignment, complex system change, culture re-creation, quality process improvements, organizational redesign, and clear strategic intent that results in significant bottom line results. Her experience includes work in over 20 countries and in all types of organizations. A believer in whole systems change, Kristine has the expertise to facilitate large groups of 1,500 as well as complex issues such as in family-owned businesses.

Recognized as the 1996 Minnesota Organization Development practitioner of the year, Kristine teaches at the Masters and Doctoral level, is a frequent presenter at the Organization Development National Conference, the International Organization Development Congress in Mexico, International Association of Facilitators, and International Management Consultants Confab.

Kristine published *The Essential Handbook: Behind the Scenes of Large Group Event* in 1996. Her other publications include *The Conscious Consultant: Mastering Change from the Inside Out* (2002) and *Organization Development At Work: Conversations on the Values, Applications, and Future of OD,* with Margaret Wheatley and Robert Tannenbaum (2004). Kristine is a co-editor for the Practicing Organization Develop Series with 13 books written by and for professional consultants and is considered to be the leading-edge information in the field of Organization Change and Development. Other publications include chapters in *Practicing Organization Development* (1995 and 2005), *The Handbook of Large Group Interventions* (2006) and articles *OD Journal* (Spring 1997) and *Organization Development Practitioner* (Vol 36, 2004)

Please visit her web site at www.DynamicalLeadership.com or contact her directly at KristineQuade@DynamicalLeadership.com

Influencing Patterns For Change:
A Human Systems Dynamics
Primer for Leaders

Foreword

Read a paper, talk to colleagues, listen to clients, and you will see how business and society are transforming. Watch leaders in the political, business, or community settings, and you'll see that leadership is transforming as well. Every day you tell and hear stories about radical surprises and unpredictable events.

It is difficult enough to observe these changes and understand them intellectually, but that is not enough for the leader. Leaders must make meaning and take action for themselves and others. It can be an overwhelming challenge to function as a transformed leader in a continually transforming environment. Wherever and however you lead, you have experienced the moment of decision and action. In the midst of a shifting landscape and changing rules, you must make a choice to move yourself and your followers forward. There was a time when experience, practice, and a delusion of control helped build the strength to face those moments of truth. These days, with change coming at us at breakneck speed, none of us has enough experience or practice or control. We must decide a course of action in a moment with limited information and unlimited options.

This book can help. It takes complex and subtle concepts from the new sciences of chaos and complexity and translates them into simple, practical tools for leaders. With true stories and practical examples, Holladay and Quade build the foundation for any leader to see and influence changing patterns of performance. They provide provocative questions for readers to challenge their own assumptions and habits. They unfold the ideas in ways that fit with individual leaders in all facets of today's communities and organizations.

I must confess: I am not an unbiased observer. Over the past twenty years I have participated in the birth of Human Systems Dynamics (HSD) and the theory and practice it engenders. Kristine and Royce have been close friends and colleagues on this journey of discovery. I am exquisitely proud of them and this work for three reasons. First, they have created a rich and accessible doorway into the fundamental principles of HSD. Second, they bring their own distinct voices to their work. Third, they continue the tradition of teaching and learning as they make each discovery an open door to the next. I hope you will join them—as a leader and a learner—in the journey of exploration and action.

Glenda H. Eoyang
Circle Pines, Minnesota
August 2008

INTRODUCTION

Who is a change leader? You could be, if you work in any organization today. Leaders come from management; they come from training programs; and they come from the ranks of committed and insightful individuals who work every day toward their organization's vision of success. You don't have to be the "boss" to use the building blocks we outline in this book. You just have to take the reins of formal or informal leadership in your area and use these principles to move forward.

Today's leaders--at all levels of the organization--find themselves in a landscape different from any that has existed for organizations in the past.

- The pace of change is faster.

- The workforce, as well as the consumer base, is more diverse and more demanding.

- Economic, social and cultural forces act at a global level, as well as local, regional and national levels.

- Information technology enables individuals to know more, do more, and communicate more than at any time in history.

- Innovation and adaptation are way of life inside today's organizations, agencies and communities.

In this new landscape, change leaders need a different set of perspectives and lenses to face their day-to-day challenges, and organizations need to respond in coherent and productive ways. This new business landscape requires adaptability, flexibility and responsiveness at the individual level, as well as at the organizational level.

The new and emerging field of Human Systems Dynamics (HSD) offers change leaders a way to look at their organizations and find the inherent creativity, energy and productivity required by organizations in today's environment. Using HSD principles, change leaders will be able to find all that in their employees at all levels and across all areas of their organizations.

This is a Primer about "letting go" of control and prediction, without abdicating the responsibilities or accountability. It is about increasing effectiveness, releasing creativity and strengthening adaptive capacity inherent in systems. It is about making decisions in consistent and coherent ways to respond to changing economic, social and cultural landscapes. It is about unleashing the system's potential.

This Primer is organized into five sections called building blocks. Each building block stands on its own or can be used in combination with the others. Woven into each building block are stories suggesting ways change leaders can use it to bring about significant change in their organizations. Each chapter ends with a set of questions to guide you in applying the building block in your own work. At the end of the Primer is an appendix that includes additional resources.

We invite you to start learning about Human Systems Dynamics and join others in gaining skills and perspectives that will bring you a greater sense of accomplishment, more appreciation for the complexity around you and an improved understanding of the dynamics in your own organization.

CHAPTER 1

WHY USE
HUMAN SYSTEMS DYNAMICS?

Human Systems Dynamics (HSD) is a new field of study and practice that provides a perspective for seeing and influencing a system in ways that more traditional approaches don't offer. HSD enables leaders to "see" and understand patterns as the underlying dynamics of their organizations to gain a clearer understanding of the challenges they face. The building blocks described here are applications from the field of HSD. They are simple and immediately actionable, and they provide multiple options to bring about change in an organization.

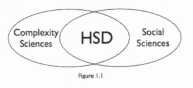

Figure 1.1

This field of study lies at the intersection where it borrows metaphors, concepts and approaches from complexity science and the social sciences. The blend of the two fields (Figure 1.1) offers elegant descriptions of the ways in which people live, work and play together in families, communities, and organizations.

Providing new perspectives and language, HSD gives change leaders ways to observe and describe what they see happening in multi-dimensional, constantly adaptive, open systems. The insights gained from HSD enable change leaders to:

- Face daily challenges of working in today's quickly changing and diverse environment,

3

- Make decisions about moving into the future with confidence,

- Bring about significant change in their organizations, and

- Sustain their organizations in ways that have not previously been considered.

How HSD is New and Different

Human Systems Dynamics (HSD) provides change leaders with a new way of understanding the nuances of thought, behavior and interaction that characterizes their organizations. Helping change leaders to see those dynamics in action, HSD differs from traditional approaches in a number of ways (see Table 1.1). The following descriptions explain each point in greater detail.

HSD Approaches	Traditional Approaches
video perspective	snapshot perspective
respond and adapt to the future	predict and control into the future
whole is greater than sum of the parts	system can be taken apart and put back together
causes are multiple and interdependent	root causes can be identified
simple rules influence complex behavior	control and mandate control behavior

Table 1.1

Change leaders watch a system over time, like a video, to understand their systems. In HSD leaders see events as emerging from the simultaneous influences over time, as opposed to independent events that "freeze" the action at some point. Through the lens of HSD, leaders understand their systems as constantly shifting and adapting to the various forces in the environment. Rather than looking at one point in time, these leaders look for meaning and progress as patterns emerge inside their organizations and beyond. This engagement and observation of the system across time helps change leaders formulate responses that are emergent and adative.

Using HSD, change leaders watch for patterns, understanding the conditions that shape emergent patterns toward desired ends or

4

influence existing patterns to amplify or damp other effects of the organization. These change leaders are sensitive to the key leverage points and multiple options for action.

They do not attempt to "freeze" their organizations to understand what is going on. They thrive in the unfolding video, the complexity of interactions, and the vibrancy of ongoing change. Change leaders who use HSD play the role of actor, director, set support and choreographer all at the same time and are comfortable moving between form and function.

Change leaders in more traditional approaches use snapshots--annual performance measures, single events and periodic feedback--to build their understandings of their systems and ensure accountability. This approach limits the change leader in two says. First a snapshot approach puts blinders on the leaders line of site. It is more difficult to see and understand relationships or to get a sense of the ongoing impact of an intervention when there is only one brief glimpse frozen in time. Second, snapshots hinder the leader's ability to respond quickly to changing forces internal or external to the organization.

Change leaders know they cannot predict the future; nor can they control how their organizations move into that future. Because systems are constantly adapting in response to multiple forces and because the future cannot be predicted with specific accuracy, neither can the system's performance in that future be predicted. Change leaders who understand HSD know that when a system-wide change is initiated, the end is unknown. Individual employees and groups of employees make choices in response to each other. Vendors and suppliers influence actions inside the organization. Customer needs drive actions from outside the organization.

Through HSD, change leaders understand they can study the patterns in their organizational systems and know, generally, how the system might respond to particular actions; they also know they cannot make specific predictions about what will happen at any given point in time in their systems.

Traditional approaches to change rely on levels and relstionship of power and control. The difficulty comes, however, when individuals, market trends, economic and social forces, and the vast diversity of today's orgainzations make control impossible. Change leaders cannot, in fact control what happens in their organizations.

Knowing that control is an illusion, change leaders use their energies in other, more productive ways to shift the conditions that influence their systems toward greater capacity and adaptability.

Organizational systems are greater than the sum of their parts.
Traditional approaches to organizational management and change suppose that a system can be broken into its component parts, and each part can be refined independently. Based in the mechanistic and "clockwork" imagery of the early 20th century, this perspective does not fit the highly volatile, quickly changing, tightly interdependent organizations required in today's landscape. This "plug and play" concept of independent organizational change is simply no longer viable.

HSD recognizes that the components across a system are interdependent, massively entangled and cannot be taken apart. Each part influences others in ways that cannot always be known. Human resources decisions can have an impact on the purchasing department. What one member brings to a team has an impact on the total team. Pressure or change in one part of the organization will cause shifts in other parts. External forces may touch different parts of the system in different ways, but those parts will, in turn, influence others.

HSD leaders look at the vertical levels of their systems to understand the whole, the part, and the greater whole, with special attention to the relationships among the levels. For example, change leaders who understand HSD know that what happens at the departmental level (whole) will impact the individuals in the department (part), as well as the total organization (greater whole). What happens at the mid-management level (whole) will impact the worker level (part) as well as top management (greater whole). No part of the organization stands alone, and HSD concepts and metaphors provide tools to help change leaders deal with the resulting messiness of change.

Changes are often the result of multiple causes. Because systems are massively entangled, there is no way to find one root cause for the challenges that emerge. What happens today in an organization may have been triggered by any number of forces acting together and on each other. What seemed to have caused today's change was, in fact, caused by other forces, which resulted from other actions and forces, which resulted from earlier actions and forces, and so on and so on and so on....

Traditional theories about organizational change look for one or more root causes. They imply that leaders should be able to pinpoint and address direct cause-effect relationships.

Because interactions and interdependencies are massively entangled, there can be no one root cause. Multiple forces are interacting whether they are seen and noticed or when they are not. Looking in only one direction or for predictable and sequential action limits change leaders' understanding of the complexities of their systems, narrows the opportunities for choice, inhibits flexibility, and reduces decision options. HSD helps change leaders see where they can influence a part to bring about change in the whole.

Complicated and coherent behavior can come from a short list of simple rules.

Considering the complexity of individual perspectives and the number of simultaneous (and possibly contradictory) activities, all of which are occurring in multiple settings in the organization, it is clear that change leaders cannot control everything all the time. Yet there remains a need for consistency and coherence in the organization. HSD uses the metaphor of short and simple rules to explain how leaders can influence coherence for organizational effectiveness, even in organizational relationships and learning that cannot be codified by procedures and policies.

Foundational Building Blocks

Based on the principles that set HSD apart from traditional ideas about organizational systems, five assumptions frame an effective approach to organizational change. Change leaders who can step into and use these perspectives are better able to influence their systems and move them toward effective and sustainable change.

- An organization is a complex system with a goal of sustaining itself by establishing patterns of responsiveness and adaptation.

- Constraints emerging from inside the system determine the type of activity and interaction that will occur in the system, requiring change leaders who are flexible and supportive.

- Systemic change occurs when the underlying dynamics of patterns are shifted to increase responsiveness and adaptation across the system.

- Simple rules guide actions and behaviors in emergent, self-organizing systems.

- A system's capacity to sustain itself depends on repeated cycles of adaptive action.

This Primer is designed to provide change leaders with a clear understanding of these assumptions so they can use them to guide actions and decisions as they increase the adaptive capacity of organizational systems. It is designed to build a foundation to help change leaders "see" the patterns moving their systems toward sustainability. Each chapter describes one HSD building block by providing a definition, a brief example of its use in an actual organizational system, suggested applications for using the building block and suggestions for its use. The following questions are explored further in each chapter.

- **Chapter 2**
  How Do I Understand My System?
  Understand how patterns emerge from interactions and then influence subsequent action in the system.

- **Chapter 3**
  How Do I Define My Role as a Change Leader?
  Understand the landscape of the organization and how to make decisions about leadership and oversight.

- **Chapter 4**
  What Difference Can I Make When I Cannot Control?
  Understand how to shift emergent patterns toward productivity and adaptation.

- **Chapter 5**
  What Informs Action When Regulations Don't Fit? Understand how to guide individual actions and decisions when the policy and procedures manual cannot cover everything.

- **Chapter 6**
  How Do I Plan in A Changing Environment?
  Understand how to use constantly emerging, unpredictable, challenging and adaptive forces in the organization for planning and formulating action.

These building blocks establish a powerful place for change leaders to stand as they move their organizations forward through complex change. Each building block is critical to the foundation, and together they form a well-grounded approach.

This Primer does not provide a "recipe" for change. Nor does it provide a step-by-step developmental approach to change. Neither of those approaches is effective at bringing about deep change in organizations, and both are mechanistic in nature. Deep change that builds the organization's capacity to respond and adapt to the multiple forces of today's environment has to be grounded in a foundation of understanding and action that shifts the underlying dynamics of these human systems.

CHAPTER 2

HOW DO I UNDERSTAND MY SYSTEM?

An organization is a complex system with a goal of sustaining itself by establishing patterns of responsiveness and adaptation.

A change leader's effectiveness lies in an ability to see the interactions in the system and the patterns that emerge from those interactions. Because of the complexity of these systems and the patterns they generate, the challenges emerging from the dynamics are particularly unique and difficult to resolve.

Sticky Issues

Some systemic challenges never seem to go away, no matter how many times they are addressed. With each new manifestation of one of these challenges, the traditional change leader steps in with the intention that, "This time it will work. This solution will make the difference, and we won't have to deal with this again!" What they find, however, is that solutions founded in the traditional, mechanistic and snapshot views of organizational change are not robust enough to address these systemic and repeating challenges.

In HSD, the recurring issues emerging from underlying dynamics of the system are referred to as "sticky issues." Unfortunately sticky issues are like glue--they hang on and are hard to clean up. They are the challenges that surface when least expected and make life difficult and daunting. Issues in one part of the organization are dealt with and suddenly the same challenge surfaces in a different part of the organization. Sticky issues never really go away--they just go "underground" and simmer in the system. Examples of sticky issues include the following.

- About the time one union group signs a contract and settles back into the work routine, the next labor group's contract is up for negotiation--over many of the same issues.

- Different groups of customers or clients demand different approaches and resolutions to their needs.

- A question of unethical reporting in the accounting area is addressed and resolved, and a month later, the research and development department is dealing with questions of ethical practice.

- Once the Board of Directors clarifies their expectations for upper management, middle management begins complaining that they are unsure of what is expected of them.

Sometimes, because of massive shifts in the environment, sticky issues might look like nothing change leaders have ever seen before.

- After September 11, 2001, many organizations had to deal with new security issues and regulations. None were simple to address. Sometimes they competed with or even contradicted established regulations and expectations; sometimes they were not articulated in ways applicable and/or usable in all settings; and sometimes they involved multiple parts of the organization in different ways.

- As technology changes and new applications and opportunities present themselves, companies re-tool or develop new ways of doing business to meet changing demands.

- The realization of a global market--even for small companies--calls for different ways of doing business. Since the global business landscape changes so rapidly, organizations continue to struggle to stay abreast of new requirements and regulations in their own fields.

- As innovations becomes a fact of life in today's business environment, organizations are forced to respond quickly and to make difficult decisions about what innovations to embrace, and which one to ignore.

These examples point to organizational dynamics sustaining the sticky issue. Old assumptions no longer apply, patterns of behavior never get addressed, lack of flexibility or adaptability render organizational structures for decision making or problem solving out of date or ineffective.

Skilled change leaders use questions to identify and understand the specific dynamics of their sticky issues. Identifying and exploring the dynamics of sticky issues inform change leaders of the nature and complexity of their issues and help them "see" the patterns more clearly. Figure 2.1. provides some general areas of focus for the change leader's questions.

- Begin by looking at all the places where the issues emerge and how large the overall impact is, looking at the whole system to see how seemingly unrelated challenges might actually be connected.

- Remain present to yesterday's challenges and how they have influenced current decisions.

- Look for similarities and differences across multiple levels, perspectives, or interconnections and how they relate to new challenges.

- Identify what is feeding an issue as it arises in different times and places across the organization.

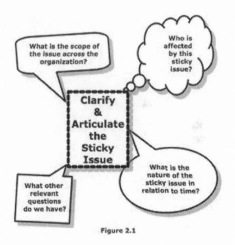

Figure 2.1

Before you move on to read about the building block, think of a sticky issue that you face and describe it in detail below. Put down as many details as you can, answering the questions listed here and in Figure 2.1.

Use the sticky issue as your own personal case study as you work with the building blocks in each of the following chapters to see how they apply in your own work. Questions have been designed to relate each building block specifically to your own sticky issues and to help you think of and work with it in a different way.

Take some time to identify your sticky Iissue before moving onto the first building block.

Sample Scope Questions:

1. Where are you seeing this issue? How many functions or departments are experiencing the same thing?

2. How many ways is this issue phrased? What are the words used to describe the same phenomena?

3. Where do processes or procedures seemed choked or constrained? Where do they seem under-constrained? What seems to be the "appropriate" level of control?

4. Is the character of the issue similar or different, depending on where it is encountered?

Sample Affect Questions:

1. How many people are experiencing this issue?

2. Does this feel like a small or large issue?

3. Does this issue seem to generate before or after other occurrences?

4. Who can and will give me more information about this issue?

Sample Nature Questions:

1. Is there a specific time element to this issue?

2. Does it appear on a regular basis?

3. Does it appear when least expected?

4. What have I learned by articulated my sticky issue?

Introduction

This building block provides a means of understanding what has always been present and what leaders have missed because they did not have the right language, experience, or set of questions to open their awareness to what was influencing their organizations.

By learning about and paying attention to patterns and how they emerge in the system, leaders can determine how to influence human systems rather than get caught up in a losing battle of attempting to predict or control them.

Description

HSD describes a complex adaptive system as a collection of semi-autonomous agents that interact in unpredictable ways that lead to system-wide patterns. These patterns, in turn, reinforce (both positively and negatively) the behaviors of the agents in the system. (Eoyang, 2001)

This definition focuses on understanding generative patterns such as competition, cooperation, trust, or excellent internal relationships. Generative patterns are described as those that build on each other, transforming with each iteration toward fitness with the greater environment.

There are also patterns that may be generative within their immediate environments, yet appear harmful in the larger context. Examples current concerns around terrorist activity and corporate greed.

- The commitment to violence and loyalty to one powerful leader are generative patterns inside the terrorist group, however those same patterns become destructive when viewed in the context of the greater world environment.

- In the corporate or non-profit setting, departments or entire organizations might choose to optimize their own work, while ignoring the impact of those decisions on the whole. While such a pattern might be beneficial to the small group, it also has the potential to be destructive when viewed in the context of the greater organizational environment.

The following series of illustrations break apart the definition of complex adaptive systems.

"Agent" refers to the individuals or individual factors making up the system being studied; they are the actors in the system. In Figures 2.2 - 2.5, the agents are people in the system. Agents can also be any of the parts of a system that interact in semi-autonomous ways.

For example, in nature ants can be the agents that work together to build their colonies. In the economy, agents can be the companies that buy and sell stocks. In the organization, the functions or departments can be the agents that create the product from design to delivery. In organizations, humans are agents who interact as they make their own decisions in the context of the organization.

Agents...

Semi-autonomous agents have some level of choice about their work. They are bound by the system, yet are still able to act on their own be half in the context of the greater whole.

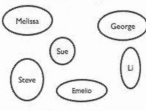

Figure 2.2

Rules--both spoken and un-spoken--help people know the difference between acceptable and unacceptable behavior. Each person in the organization has a choice about whether or not to follow these rules in their own behaviors. Each person knows his or her relative success may depend on complying with those rules, but they still have the choice to comply.

Interact...

Over time, these semi-autonomous agents interact with each other in multiple ways. They are interdependent in their work and work-place social structure. (Figure 2.3) One person's work products become the raw materials for the next person's activities. Ideas are shared and expanded. People celebrate successes and mourn losses. They learn and grow together in healthy organizations. Their ongoing interactions create day-to-day relationships; their interactions accomplish the work of the organization; and their interactions have multiple impacts on other members of the workforce and on the customer base.

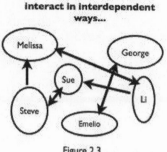

interact in interdependent ways...

Figure 2.3

The multiple and varied interactions between and among the agents in a system begin to generate system-wide patterns. For example, if the system is the stock market, the individual agents are stocks and brokers. The term "bullish market" refers to a system-wide pattern where the stocks are performing well and the brokers are buying and selling at a high rate and at a profit.

Form Patterns...

"Patterns" are similarities and differences that have meaning across space and time. Behaviors and relationships among agents who work together build shared meaning over time and show up as patterns of interaction across the system.

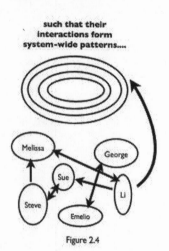

such that their interactions form system-wide patterns....

Figure 2.4

In human systems, a system-wide pattern reflects the ways in which individuals interact with each other. Depending on specific behaviors in the system, different patterns will emerge. If the individuals in figure 2.4 interact in ways that support diversity and self-expression, they establish a pattern of tolerance that may come to characterize their system. Patterns of competition and isolation will emerge when individuals interact in secretive and competitive ways.

Patterns Reinforce the System...

New employees, who were not a part of the original interactions, are influenced by patterns and their learned behavior helps them fit in and be successful. The patterns often become codified in organizational policies and practices that outline what gets rewarded or amplified in the system, and what gets ignored or damped, as depicted in Figure 2.5.

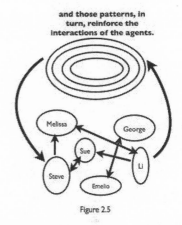

and those patterns, in turn, reinforce the interactions of the agents.

Figure 2.5

This is how organizational culture develops and is institutionalized. The observable patterns of interaction--both spoken and unspoken--emerge from the day-to-day behaviors and interactions of the people in the system, and subsequently guide behaviors of individuals. Leaders who want to change the culture of an organization break old patterns of interaction and reinforce new patterns that characterize the culture they want to establish.

Other examples of patterns in complex adaptive systems:

- Buying and selling products or services create trends that, in turn, influence how others buy and sell.

- Ideas and experiences establish perspectives that influence how to see the world and gain additional insights.

- Businesses compete and establish market niches, which influence decisions about new products, customer service and advertising.

Purpose

The purpose of this building block is to help change leaders identify patterns that move a complex adaptive system toward fit in its environment. "Fit" describes the degree to which a system is able to survive (sustain in its environment). The patterns that emerge inside an organization should contribute to its fitness.

Good customer service, responsive innovation, and ethical practice are all examples of patterns that are most likely to move a system toward fitness over the long term. Organizations will sometimes be able to thrive during the short term with patterns that do not fit into the greater whole, as in the Enron scandal. Over time what was profitable for a few individuals was shown to be disastrous for the organization.

Complex issues and opportunities cannot be understood or solved with traditional problem-solving methods. Understanding challenges as sticky issues and looking for the patterns that give rise to those issues provide a way to work more effectively in a complex adaptive system.

Example

Situation and Opportunity

In a financial organization, the new CEO, Betty, wanted to establish a strong sense of ethical behavior and collaboration between and among the employees. The predecessor was a person who had encouraged competition and had created barriers between departments and smaller units, developing elaborate and complicated schemes of recognition, reward and even punishment to maintain the separation and competition between units.

As she entered the organization, Betty talked with each board member, a number of current and former clients, formal and informal leaders inside the organization, and other employees at all levels of the organization. What she realized was, almost without exception, people were tired of the highly competitive environment, and they were leery of the unethical behavior that had emerged as a result of those patterns.

Because she understood the nature of a complex adaptive system, Betty knew that well-intentioned employees and board members were influenced by counterproductive patterns established by her predecessor. She saw her actions in the first few months as her greatest opportunity to influence those patterns.

Action

Over time, Betty used different ways of talking about these issues. Her first speech to employees communicated her vision of collaboration and ethical behavior. Newsletters quoted what was important to her. She formed a representative team from across the organization, and included board members and clients to create a set of simple rules to clarify her intentions.

Betty and her leadership team eliminated the schemes for rewarding competition and replaced them with recognition and celebration of collaboration among and between departments. She also reorganized the company into cross-functional teams that served all the needs of a client in one place, rather than in silos across the organization. Finally, she worked with others to institute a system of checks and balances to ensure a greater level of accountability for ethical action. Throughout this entry process, Betty modeled the collaborative patterns she wanted to see across the organization.

With her top management, Betty worked to institute an ongoing process of evaluation and accountability that constantly scanned the organization and tracked the patterns of behavior as they emerged. When they saw anything violating the patterns they were shaping for collaboration and ethics, they took steps to correct the system's course and re-align with the vision of cooperation and ethical behavior.

Result

As a result of Betty's actions, the organization regained clients lost under previous management and a renewed sense of energy and commitment emerged among employees. The company has continued to grow.

Anyone might ask how this process was different from a leader who did not know anything about complex adaptive systems. It might not be any different. Because the metaphors and concepts of HSD come from studying nature and natural systems, they are highly intuitive. Many strong leaders take steps they believe will move their systems forward, even though they do not have a theory base that tells them why their intuitions make such good sense. In this case, however, Betty's understanding of the complexity of her organization helped her know what she was looking for, informed her questions and analysis, and helped her formulate effective options for action. She, like any change leader who knows HSD, was able to work in intentional and meaningful ways because she understood how her system worked.

When to Use or Not Use This Building Block

Understanding complex adaptive systems will help change leaders "know" their organizations in new ways. The concept of complex adaptive systems is most effective for understanding large, system-wide challenges, such as sticky issues. One reminder for change leaders is to notice procedural or simple challenges that continue to arise over time. When these small issues begin to happen frequently, change leaders can

look at the patterns to try to analyze the systemic source in the underlying dynamics of the organization.

Tips and Traps

- Effective change leaders remember that the meaning they assign to
  any pattern is their own meaning. They do not rely on just one perspective to develop full understanding. They realize they should
  check their perceptions and see what others are thinking as well.

- One large, underlying sticky issue may emerge as smaller, seemingly less complex challenges in different parts of the organization.
  Great change leaders look across the system to know what is
  emerging and watch for patterns in those emergent issues.

- Individual people, generally, are likely to perform as well or as
  badly as the system in which they work. If an individual's performance is struggling, it may be a system issue. If several individuals are experiencing similar performance challenges, it is
  highly likely that there is a pattern in the system that needs to be
  addressed. Highly effective change leaders look to the system first
  to identify sources of performance challenges.

This building block can help with sticky issues by unfolding the patterns that contribute to the complexity of the issue.

Think about your own sticky issue to see how it emerges from your complex adaptive system.

Sample Scope Questions:

1. How are the policies or procedures applied similarly or differently, depending on the department, group or level in the organization?

2. What causes more rigorous attention in some parts of the organization or with some groups and not others?

3. Are there different approaches to problem solving, some working and some not?

Sample Affect Questions:

1. Who are the people (agents) and how are they interacting with each other?

2. How would you characterize patterns that are emerging from their interactions?

3. What are you noticing about interactions in the world outside the system?

4. What expectations (explicit or implicit) are being established for how people interact?

Sample Nature Questions:

1. How would you describe the agents at work in this system?

2. What is the observable challenge that emerges from these agents?

3. How would you describe the emergent patterns?

4. In what ways is this establishing expectations or influencing how the system will behave in the future?

CHAPTER 3

HOW DO I DEFINE MY ROLE
AS A CHANGE LEADER?

Constraints emerging from inside the system determine the type of activity and interaction that will occur, requiring change leaders who are flexible and supportive.

This question about role is very often the first question change leaders ask. While knowing they can neither control nor predict the complex interactions of their systems, they know some processes and procedures have to be predictable and controllable. Payroll and accounting are the most common examples used, and many areas of business need a high level of internal control. At the same time, in a complex adaptive system, there are places where such a high level of control is neither productive nor adaptive. For example, research and development functions within the organization need greater freedom to explore and identify trends and new technologies, calling for less control.

Individuals who respond to complex customer issues require greater freedom to respond to varying needs most appropriately. Supervisors need greater freedom to respond to the needs of their employees.

There exists, in any organization, points where learning happens, where relationships form, where people are asked to make split-second decisions in situations that might not fit the specifics of a policy or procedure. New ideas emerge in response to new questions. Someone has to be vigilant in the external environment and watch emergent trends that may have an impact on the organization. These types of activities cannot be regulated or codified.

So what does this say about the role of the change leader? If parts of the system cannot or should not be controlled, what can a change leader do? If an activity is out of the range of control, it is just chaos? How does the change leader know where to control and where not to control? Are those two ends of the polarity--control and not control--the only options for the effective change leader?

The next building block, the Landscape Diagram, helps change leaders understand systems in a way that increases their abilities to navigate these levels of ambiguity. The organization is pictured as a landscape where multiple forces elicit differing responses. By using this diagram as a map, change leaders can better understand the needs of their systems and define their own roles in supporting the organization's growth.

The Landscape Diagram can help change leaders understand their sticky issues by using specific questions.

• Where does the sticky issue lie on the diagram?

• What can be learned about the sticky issue from understanding the zones of the landscape?

• What skills or insights can be drawn from the Landscape Diagram that will help address the sticky issue?

Introduction

In reality, work in organizations can be characterized along a scale from tightly organized to highly unorganized in its daily activities, requiring varying levels of control and/or management, depending the specific situation and job to be accomplished. For change leaders, a difficulty lies in the fact that most traditional management theories present the workplace and the role of leader as always in control--always knowing exactly what to do and how to do it. In a system that is constantly adapting to changes in its environment, this level of control throughout simply is not possible.

The Landscape Diagram is one of the change leader's building blocks that provides a graphic representation of this continuum of activity and guides decisions about what to do as the system moves along the continuum.

Description

The Landscape Diagram is a simple graph that provides a picture of the "lay of the land" in organizational work. It is designed to illustrate the necessary differences in activity across an adaptive system and provides a way to "see" the patterns that form in the organization as people shift between agreement and certainty. It is most efficient to think of the diagram as an open system, with no clear lines of transition, where people, information and work flow (See Figure 3.1)

When considering any question or action, two dimensions influence how people approach the challenge--agreement and certainty.

- **"Agreement"** refers to the degree to which people involved agree on the actions to take, or the degree to which processes and procedures are mutually supportive. Descriptions can be anywhere on a continuum from "close to" agreement to "far from" agreement, as indicated on the Y-axis.

29

- **"Certainty"** refers to the degree with which people can be sure about what is going to happen or the degree to which processes and procedures are clear enough to ensure that something will happen according to design. Again, the degree can range from "close to" certainty to "far from" certainty, as indicated on the X-axis.

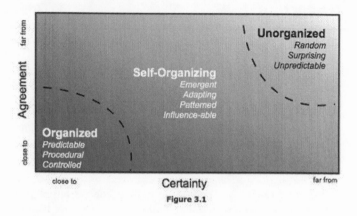

Figure 3.1

In any given situation, both dimensions are at play. When people or processes are close to agreement and close to certainty, work is organized, predictable and controlled. This area on the Landscape Diagram is referred to as the **"Organized Zone."** Some functions in organizational life require these conditions in order to to function successfully.

Payroll is the example used earlier. The payroll process has to be designed to accomplish the task as efficiently and effectively as possible. People have to be in agreement about what to do to get their time sheets turned in and how to get their checks. Additionally a strong degree of certainty must exist about when the paychecks will be distributed.

Other examples of functions that require high agreement and high certainty include manufacturing, technical work and surgery. Change leaders whose work lies in the Organized Zone are effective when they use approaches that make expectations clear and maintain lowest levels of variation.

At the other end of the spectrum, there are times when events are "far from" certainty and agreement. In the flu season, there is no way to predict who or how many people will call in sick. Customer calls are unpredictable; every time a customer calls the customer service line, it's a new call. These are examples of situations that are more chaotic,

30

unorganized and unpredictable, leading to the label of **"Unorganized Zone."** In this zone, there are no patterns to observe.

What change leaders see, when they pay attention in the Unorganized Zone, are the emergence of trends, as similar events and situations begin to repeat themselves. Knowing their role is to be present, change leaders watch for possible trends in the complexity, both inside and outside their organizations so they can respond appropriately, keep information flowing, connect networks, and maintain a sense of humor. They watch for trends that are important to the system and identify ways to amplify those trends, creating patterns that shift activity out of the Organized Zone to greater levels of organization. Finally they watch for trends that can be detrimental to the system and identify ways to damp those. External trends might be new technologies, shifts in customer needs or wants or emerging law or public policy that will affect the organization. Internal trends can be increased absenteeism, costs that continue to creep up quarter after quarter, or increasing creativity in innovation and problem solving.

In the **"Self-Organizing Zone,"** patterns and relationships emerge as agents respond to each other and as the system responds to its environment. These patterns and relationships, may come to characterize the system, or they may be short-lived. Patterns and relationships are still far enough from agreement and certainty that specific rules and regulations can't be applied. What happens may or may not have happened before, and the organization has to be able to respond in adaptive and flexible ways.

All relationships, learning, and growth happen in this emergent space because there is "give-and-take" in all interactions. This zone is where change leaders must first identify those patterns of behavior and interchange that move the organization forward, and then respond in productive ways that help the organization adapt to the environment. They must also find ways to damp those patterns of behavior that are detrimental to the organization.

Purpose

The purpose of the Landscape Diagram is to provide change leaders with the understanding they need to support and value appropriate patterns occurring in each of the three zones of any organizational culture: Organized, Self-Organizing and Unorganized. Understanding the characteristics of all three and how they work together allows leaders and individuals to recognize all areas of the organizational landscape and to appreciate the contributions of each.

The Landscape Diagram is useful at the personal level, as well as at the systems and process levels. For example, the research and development process is unorganized in the beginning. Ideas and responses emerge in the Unorganized Zone and are captured by those individuals who are looking for new ideas. As those ideas become more fully formed, they emerge as patterns that can be influenced and explored as prototypes and plans in the Self-Organizing Zone. Finally in the Organized Zone the ideas and plans take on the specifications required by standardized manufacturing and implementation.

On a personal level, different people respond to their worlds differently. Some people prefer predictability and control, others prefer freedom of adaptation and response and others prefer the free-wheeling spontaneity of the unorganized landscape. Conflicts emerge as people interact out of a lack of understanding of these differences and their impacts on personal behavior. Manufacturing people cannot understand why the research people bring them ideas that have not considered the concept's full impact, such as possible re-tooling of existing systems, material requirements, or cost. Research staff feel stifled when their ideas are "shot down" by the manufacturing or accounting department for considering what they see as only the present-time impact, while not looking at the long-term benefits.

The Landscape Diagram allows change leaders to understand the organization's internal system as well as the greater system beyond the organization's external boundary. Internally the Landscape Diagram helps change leaders see and understand the relationships and adaptations of individuals and processes across internal organizational boundaries. Reporting relationships, role clarity, respect for other viewpoints, processes and procedures are all internal issues that can be examined using the Landscape Diagram.

Externally, the Landscape Diagram can help create a picture of how the organization is adapting to its greater environment. At this scale, change leaders can examine how the organization is competing in the market, how creatively it is able to respond to external challenges, how well it gathers and uses information about customers, vendors, and other external factors and their significant impacts on the organization's performance.

Applications

Movement on the Landscape

Activities, events, or projects often move across the landscape as they shift between levels of certainty and agreement. What was once an odd occurrence is now an everyday event, as expectations and rituals get attached to it inside the organization. When new products are created, they move from random ideas into the self-organizing process of design and development into the organized world of production, which is close to certainty and close to agreement.

No one area of the landscape is inherently better than the others--there is nothing "naughty or nice" about being in the Organized, Self-Organizing, or Unorganized Zones. What is important is nurturing and amplifying behavior that brings about the greatest fit for the system at any given time.

Activity shifts on the Landscape Diagram according to the degrees of freedom required. Activity requiring increased degrees of freedom moves toward the Unorganized Zone. For example, if a set process is not working as well as it should, those assigned to fix it remove the limits of the old process, shifting the work to the Self-Organizing Zone, where they try new approaches and steps. Then, as they re-establish and redefine the process, it shifts again toward the Organized Zone. (See Figure 3.2)

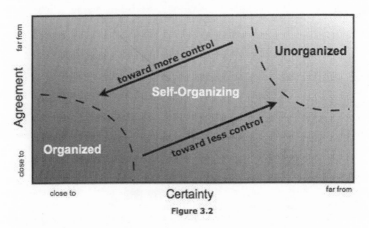

Figure 3.2

There are many ways this can be observed in an organization.

• As individuals learn, they explore new ideas that emerge in the Unorganized Zone. As the individuals pull those ideas together, concepts get formed as meaning emerges in the context of the individuals' lives and work--the ideas begin to self-organize. With practice and further reflection, the concepts formalize as ways to guide individual behaviors or decisions. The formal processes and expectations shift the work closer to certainty and agreement, moving it into the Organized Zone.

- When people are assigned to teams, they generally come together as "unknowns" to each other. Even if they have worked together in prior situations, each of them brings different perceptions and approaches to the purpose of the team (Unorganized Zone). Over time, as the team matures, the individuals begin to build common understandings about what each person brings, about the purpose of the team and about how the work needs to be accomplished (Self-Organizing Zone). Eventually, expectations and understandings begin to govern interactions of team members and move them toward greater agreement and certainty (Organized Zone). As mutual expectations--group agreements--move them toward greater agreement and certainty in their relationships, their actual work--developing new products, designing training, or scanning the environment--may remain further from certainty and agreement.

- New employees enter the workplace with little or no real understanding of patterns of behavior governing interactions and work (Unorganized Zone). They learn from others which behaviors are acceptable and rewarded and which behaviors are not allowed. They make their own choices about their actions, and as their perspectives move toward greater agreement and certainty within the context of the overall expectations (Self-Organizing Zone), they begin to fit in the overall scheme of workplace norms and culture (Organized Zone).

Constraints in the System

Constraints represent degrees of freedom that emerge from within the system. High constraints provide few degrees of freedom; low constraints increase the degrees of freedom. The Organized Zone represents high levels of constraint; the Unorganized Zone represents low levels of constraint. Strong change leaders recognize that constraints emerge from inside the system. Rules and regulations, expectations and norms, attitudes and commitment represent some constraints that occur in a system and effect it. To move a concept toward greater agreement and certainty, change leaders find ways to the increase the constraints around it.

Each of the examples below reflects this move toward greater constraint, as shown in Figure 3.3.

- Individuals move from a general exploration of new ideas to formal concepts by the meaning they make as they bring new ideas together. Sometimes a group might find themselves simply stewing around in new ideas, with little shared meaning or progress toward

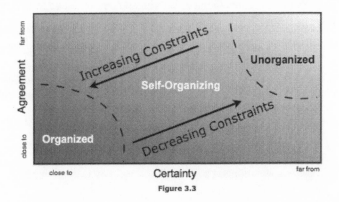

Figure 3.3

a stated goal. The change leader can help the members of the group move forward by increasing constraint in different ways, such as by reinforcing the goal, by establishing time limits, or by limiting their resources for gaining new information.

- Shared expectations and goals emerge in a team to constrain the actions of the individuals by creating clarity around how their own actions contribute to or disrupt the work of the whole team. Sometimes one member still remains oblivious to his or her impact on a group. The change leader then can add constraints by shorter feedback loops that link actions or behavior closer to the time of impact, in such a way the member is able to understand the situation and shift his/her behavior appropriately.

- As employees enter a new workplace and learn about how to fit in, their behavior becomes more constrained by the norms and expectations of the existing culture. Change leaders can increase constraints to make this transition easier, by assigning a mentor who communicates closely and frequently with the new employee or by providing in-depth training and orientation before the individual even starts his/her official duties. Many companies provide a new-hire orientation to help employees understand the organizational culture, expectations, history and values before the employees start work.

- If a change leader sees that rumors in the system are running rampant, he or she might create a constraint by increasing communications--providing more frequent, targeted, or varied formats. By putting those constraints on his or her own communications, a change leader can increase the accurate information available to the system, often decreasing the need for new rumors and dispelling those that currently exist.

35

Conversely, change leaders can allow for greater freedom of movement and adaptability by reducing the constraints that exist.

- When increased creativity is the goal, change leaders decrease the constraints by engaging others in brainstorming and by asking "What if..." questions to help people think "outside the box."

- As new employees gain skill and move past their probationary status, the constraints decrease--greater freedom in decision making, removal of probationary status, distancing of mentors--giving the employees greater freedom and broader ranges of responsibility.

- When a team falls into "group think," the constraints of old, shared thinking can be reduced by the addition of new team members.

Activities in the Zones

Each of the zones of the Landscape Diagram is important to the overall functioning of the system. All must be considered all the time. They each bring a value to the system, but each zone can also be disruptive if there is not a match between the required outcomes of an activity and the zone in which it occurs.

Remember that movement between the Zones is defined by the constraints (degrees of freedom) that give rise to and support the degree of certainty and agreement in the system.

- Activity in the Unorganized Zone is characterized by few or no constraints relative to the system. When the system needs new ideas, when there is a need to know what is happening outside the system or when change leaders watch for possible emergent trends inside the system, individuals have to think beyond the constraints that hold the system together. Einstein's famous quote about not being able to "solve problems from the same mindset that created them" speaks to this. If change leaders want to bring in new ideas, if they want to find truly innovative solutions, if they want to gain a real understanding about their customers' needs, they will develop ways of listening and collecting information that are not constrained by the current thinking in the system. When responses are characterized by ideas like, "That's not how we do it around here," the system is too constrained and does not allow the rich exploration that can happen in the Unorganized Zone.

- In the Self-Organizing Zone, activity is characterized by constraints that allow for meaning making and adaptation. The purpose of self-organization in nature is to adapt and find fit in the environment. There must be enough constraints that the boundaries and purposes of the system are clear, yet constraints must also allow the organization to try new ways, adapt to changing demands and shift toward greater fit and sustainability in the greater environment.

- The Organized Zone is where the system establishes the greatest degree of constraint. The constraints come from commonalities in the system that allow for members of the system to be close to agreement and close to certainty. Rules, regulations, processes, procedures and policies constrain the organization in a way that saves system energy by eliminating guesswork or trial and error.

Understanding that people, tasks, and thinking shift on the landscape according to the constraints that exist and knowing what types of leadership and support people need in each area can provide powerful insights for change leaders as they support staff and work in all three areas.

Uses

The Landscape Diagram helps change leaders understand that the challenges they face are sometimes about

- Processes and procedures that they can control;
- Events and situations they can't control, but can influence toward greater adaptive capacity; and
- Watching changes and patterns that cannot be controlled or influenced and responding in adaptive and productive ways.

The Landscape Diagram can be used in a number of ways.

- It can became the centerpiece of a retreat, triggering conversations about next steps, organizational and personal needs and long-range planning.
- It is useful as a framework to sort out frustration about levels of uncertainty.
- It provides a powerful foundation for discussions about leadership roles and styles.
- It can trigger or support conversation about roles or how to maximize contributions toward greater outcomes.
- It can be used to analyze and assess a current situation, to manage group interactions and to plan a project or instructional experience.

Example

Situation

ABC Corporation provides technical services to customers in a highly regulated industry. They identify themselves as the insurance for systems staying accurate and active. The prior CEO came from the operations function and operated according to the mantra, "failure is not an option". Everyone viewed this mantra as setting a high bar for customer service. The new CEO of ABC Corporation was promoted from the marketing function and wanted to expand service to other industries and sectors. He and his direct reports crafted six management principles to provide guidance during this expansion. Every manager was required to attend one of ten sessions offered globally for discussion about the meaning of the principles and how managers could bring them to life in their various areas.

Opportunity

Included in the design of the sessions was a discussion about the Landscape Diagram. Three phases of discussions were facilitated. The first phase was designed to help management team members understand that their organization was shifting from the Organized Zone out to the Unorganized Zone, based on the shift in focus away from "failure is not an option" to six principles that were less concrete and specific. During this discussion, managers took steps to make the principles more concrete as they formulated examples of what it would look like if the principles were practiced in their daily work. This discussion provided meaning and moved them, as a team of managers, into the Self-Organizing zone at different paces and through different means.

The second phase of the discussion led the managers to discuss identified individual preferences along the Diagram and where a predominance of their work actually occurred. The Operations managers could see their work mainly in the Organized Zone, where technical systems required accuracy and accountability. The Marketing managers could see their work was more externally focused on the ever-expanding needs and expectations of customers, which placed it generally in the Unorganized Zone.

During the final set of discussions, the managers looked at how they could use this new understanding to work together more effectively.

Action

Each of the sessions generated a definition for each of the six principles--as understood by the managers attending that session. The definitions were then shared with managers attending other sessions. Early in the process, one of the principles did not make sense as written, and the managers were able to craft a new way of phrasing the principle for greater clarity and agreement. The robust definitions created appropriate constraints to allow the managers to see the principles as guidelines for actions rather than commands for precise performance.

In addition, managers were able to identify unified talking points for what the principles would mean to each employee and how each work group would have an opportunity to work with and understand each principle, much the same way the managers had during their process.

The managers could see how their personal preferences and work assignment provided a different perspective, depending on the Zone where their work was centered. Knowing this, they were able to consider how their staff staff members would respond differently, depending on personal preference and work assignment. Each manager formulated discussion points for the principles and how they would be used to guide decisions in their own areas of responsibility.

Results

The process of coming to understand the new principles through the lens of the Landscape Diagram enabled a number of organizational changes designed to increase effectiveness and productivity.

- Selection of problem-solving teams now include the criteria of balance of members with preference and work skills across the Landscape Diagram to ensure differences of perspectives and approaches.

- As cross functional-teams convene, they first discuss personal preference and work assignments based on the Landscape Diagram Zones. Teams organize more quickly and effectively because of this framing.

- Managers designed their own performance evaluation measures, using the definitions of the principles. The performance measures take into account how each principle might be demonstrated differently, depending on the type of work.

- A peer-to-peer feedback process was established for managers to acknowledge appropriate application of the principles as well as Landscape Diagram preference and work assignment.

- The management team used the descriptions of the Landscape Diagram to assess appropriate assignments for new managers-- looking for fitness of preference, work requirements and balance for the entire team.

When to Use or Not Use This Building Block

When to Use

- Use this building block when change leaders are attempting to control everything and feeling frustrated that they cannot be successful. Developing a picture of the system as complex can help them understand they cannot control everything. It helps move the approach from what can be controlled to questions about what they can influence and how.

- When activities are leaving no room for adaptive change in the organization, use this tool to show a need for the system to remove constraints and move toward the Self-Organizing Zone.

- When a group shows signs of burnout or being "stuck" too long, this building block reveals other types of tasks to be accomplished or approaches to consider to shift the constraints.

- When the group feels confused and out of control, this building block helps members "see" where they are and either acknowledge that or move to a place that is more comfortable to them.

- When the change leader is unable to see the greater whole, use this building block to help him or her find a place to stand and understand the whole and the relationships among the parts.

When Not to Use

While understanding the reality of an organization is always a "plus," there are times when this building block is more useful than others. It is less useful when individuals are comfortable with their relative roles and there is not a problem of over- or under-control in the group.

It is less useful for organizations already appropriately constrained and able to respond and adapt to the challenges it faces.

Tip and Traps

- Group members can identify their group task or actions on the Landscape Diagram in multiple places at the same time. The Diagram does not describe a linear process or system where everything is orderly and predictable and the progress from one Zone to another is smooth.

- Members of the organization are able to see their dependency on each other to perform activities or accomplish goals. No one place on the landscape is any better or worse than any other; each contributes to the overall ability of the organization to adapt creatively and thrive. Great change leaders are constantly vigilant about the level of constraints that exist and their fit for the purposes of the organization.

- Some activities in the organization are more controllable--closer to agreement and certainty--than others. Change leaders understand this and establish and maintain constraints appropriately.

- The Landscape Diagram is not just a categorization schema. To think of it as simply a way to categorize the work of parts of the organization is to miss the richness that is available in understanding it as a continuum of action and response that allows for adaptation to challenges as they emerge in the environment.

- When a new issue is presented to an individual or group, they will move to the Unorganized Zone as they experience disorientation caused by new information, approaches or actions. As the individual or group begins to make sense of the issue, they move into the Self-Organizing Zone and begin to make meaning of the new ideas and develop patterns of thought and response to it. Once the individual or group has developed a formalized action, they will be operating from the Organized Zone.

Thinking about your own sticky issue, respond to the following questions.

1. Where do the main challenges of your sticky issue lie on the Landscape Diagram?

2. How much of your challenge is related to the self-organizing relationships between and among individuals? What are the constraints (or lack of constraints) that might be impeding the work that needs to be done? What are some ways you can shift constraints to encourage more functional relationships?

3. Beyond individual relationships, do you believe that your sticky issue is a result of over constraint or under constraint in your system? What (if any) constraints do you see that are pushing the situation too far toward the Organized Zone? What (if any) constraints would bring it further toward agreement and certainty, if that is the problem?

CHAPTER 4

WHAT DIFFERENCE CAN I MAKE WHEN I CANNOT CONTROL?

Systemic change occurs when the underlying dynamics of patterns are shifted to increase responsiveness and adaptation across the system.

In the Organized Zone of the Landscape Diagram, high levels of agreement and certainty result from constraints that reduce the degrees of freedom in the system. Change leaders can and do establish constraints by using procedures, rules and other expectations to control behavior and interactions.

There is a need sometimes, however, for the system to be less constrained to allow it to create the appropriate responses and adapt to an unpredictable environment. In the Self-Organizing Zone, leaders cannot control every interaction, nor can they predict, either at the individual or at the system level.

That does not mean that the change leader has no role in shaping individual and organizational responses. Glenda Eoyang, through her research in organizations, has identified three conditions that influence how self-organization takes place in a complex adaptive system.

In this building block, the Eoyang CDE Model defines the conditions that must be present for the organizing process. Change leaders use this building block to become aware of and understand their systems. This

43

level of understanding then enables them to use those conditions to influence system change.

The Eoyang CDE Model can help change leaders think about their sticky issues and how the conditions in their systems contribute to the challenges they face. They can then begin to think about how to shift those conditions to increase the adaptive capacity of their organizations.

Introduction

In a complex adaptive system, most of the experiences of change leaders are represented by the Self-Organizing Zone of the Landscape Diagram. In this Zone, they cannot legislate or codify all answers or situations. How do they know what to do when they can neither control nor predict? How do they create the patterns they want in their organizations when those patterns emerge only when there are fewer constraints? How do they amplify those patterns they want to increase and how do they damp those patterns they want to eliminate?

The Eoyang CDE Model offers options for influencing the patterns characterizing an organization. She names three conditions that leaders can use to shift the conditions of self-organization in their systems.

- Containers
- Differences
- Exchanges

Description

The Eoyang CDE Model names conditions that influence the speed, path, and direction of pattern formation in all areas of the organization. The conditions may be more or less constrained across the system, placing them in all Zones represented on the Landscape Diagram.

Containers

Containers establish the boundaries of the system until the pattern can emerge and take form. Within each type of container, examples have been listed, but the possibilities are almost endless.

- Physical – delineates what is allowed in and what is kept out. Examples include buildings, cubicles or offices, meeting spaces, executive floors and high security work spaces.

- **Organizational** – refers to what you see on an organizational chart or in family or community groupings. Examples include departments, divisions, sisters and brothers, neighborhoods, denominations, political parties and professional associations.

- **Conceptual or psychological** – refers to what will draw people together or attract them into affinity groups, hobbies or beliefs. Examples include an organization's vision or mission, the strategic direction of the organization, a set of procedures, a charismatic leader, a religious deity and a bonus for work performed. These containers also refer to affinities within the organization because of the boundaries formed according to similar likes and dislikes among a group of individuals.

Any number of containers can exist in a system at any given time. For instance, in one building there may be a number of departments of one organization. Within that department, there might be groups of men, women, young employees, experienced employees, salaried employees, hourly workers. Additionally the individuals might belong to containers according to their faith preferences, type of school or education, what approach they take to the work, and a multitude of other factors.

Containers can be highly constrained--as they are in the Organized Zone--or they can be less constrained--as in the Self-Organizing Zone and in the Unorganized Zone.

Differences

Differences manifest the patterns in the system by allowing the potential for movement or change across the organization. When you look at patterned fabric, it is the differences of shape and color that make it interesting. The same is true in an organization. It is the differences among the agents in the system that create the patterns. Those differences may be personal and individual, such as work style or how each person establishes a relationship. The differences may be at the organizational level, such as the differences between the research and development function and the production function. Or they may be more global, such as buying patterns dependent on regional or national holidays.

Whatever the number or scale of the differences, they provide the potential for complementary action or for conflict. Change leaders watch for differences, know which ones create the greatest impact, and understand how to take appropriate action accordingly.

The number and types of difference in a system can be many. Some examples include the following.

- Stylistic - a preferred way an individual or group may perform and function or see their world.

- Background - the history or experiences that members bring to work.

- Outlook - the meaning assigned and the conscious or unconscious philosophy which drives this meaning-making process.

Differences manifest in a system in two ways: by the number of differences that exist in the system and by degree of difference in any one element. For instance, as a team comes together the differences may be constrained by the scope of experiences among the members. They may have experiences as leaders, in other organizations, at national or global levels, or in other roles in the organization. On the other hand, the differences may be constrained by the level and ability in one area of difference. For example there may be a difference in the degree of leadership skill that each person exhibits.

Exchanges

Exchanges are the ways a system connects to itself or its environment to share time, energy, information, and other resources. Exchanges can be language-based (talking and listening, email, newsletters, phone communications), they can be a source of organizational culture and expectations (job descriptions, data and feedback, rules and regulations), or they can be a movement of resources that support the organization's work (salary, time assignments, budget allocations). Change leaders use exchanges to collect and share the information and resources that are most important to the survival of the organization. Exchanges occur at all levels in the organization and support or create change by informing patterns in the system. They are generally the most accessible avenue for understanding what makes an organization tick.

Purpose and Application

The Eoyang CDE Model allows leaders to understand, name and influence patterns. This powerful model helps change leaders:

- Be aware of the system and observe the underlying dynamics,

- Analyze the system to understand what is happening from a different perspective, and

- Influence the system by taking steps to constrain or loosen the containers, differences or exchanges.

Be Aware of the System

This is the first step toward being able to understand and influence the system. In any given situation leaders can use a table like Table 4.1 below to identify the containers (C), differences (D), and exchanges (E) that are relevant to an issue that is important to them, a challenge they face or a problem they want to solve.

Containers	Differences	Exchanges

Table 4.1

Analyze the System

Once change leaders have a good idea of the relevant containers, differences, and exchanges, they can see if the system is appropriately constrained. Constraints limit the activities of the agents in the system, and understanding them is important. By themselves, constraints are neither "naughty nor nice." They just are. Limits are necessary to differing degrees in a system and the only judgment to be made is whether or not the constraints allow the system to self-organize toward fit or sustainability in the environment.

In seeing and analyzing a system it is important to be able to see the constraints and make appropriate choices about how to increase or decrease constraints appropriately. Systems that are overly constrained make events happen too quickly, limit creativity or exploration and increase conflict in the system. When a system is under constrained, it is too random, patterns cannot emerge, and conflicts increase. Change leaders gather information from the system to judge the level of constraints. By using the CDE chart represented in Table 4.1 as a resource, leaders can examine each of the containers, differences and exchanges to determine the level of constraint.

Influence the System

Once change leaders have identified the containers, differences and exchanges that are relevant to their particular issues and the constraints involved, they can determine whether the constraints are appropriate to allow for successful functioning of the system. If they are not, change leaders can intervene by shifting any of the conditions. Figure 4.1 shows how shifting each condition will impact the constraints.

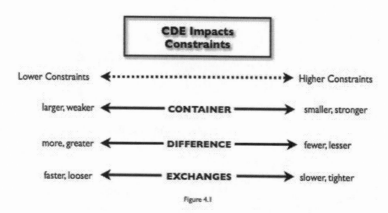

Figure 4.1

Container Interventions

Containers bound the system until system-wide patterns emerge. The container brings individuals or agents together so they can interact in ways that generate recognizable system-wide patterns. At the beginning of a meeting, people begin to gather, and there is no structure. When the group begins the work, the agenda constrains attention toward a common objective or goal. Members of the group have roles, such as the facilitator who influences the participation in the meeting. The recorder documents the discussion. The group may function one way if the meetings are "stand up" and fast by design (less constrained) or "sit down" and longer with a complex agenda (more constrained).

In real life there are many containers in operation at once, and they are massively entangled. For example, one person can be a member of a task team, the work group, a social group, and the larger department. The container can be considered large (loosely bounded with few constraints) or small (tightly bounded with larger or more constraints). If there are rules that guide behavior, these might be a way of tightening the container (greater constraint). If there are only simple guidelines, these might be considered a way to loosen the container and provide options for more interplay (looser constraints).

To think about how they need to influence these containers change leaders might consider diagnostic questions like the following.

- What are the current relevant containers?

- Are they physical, organizational, or conceptual?

- Is the problem coming up because the container is too large or too small?

- Are the constraints too great or to small?

- How might I shift the container to get the activities I want?

- What do I want to accomplish by shifting the container?

- What might be at risk when changing the container?

- What will I watch for as the container is changed?

Once they understand the constraints and the conditions that are at play, a change leader has a number of options available for ways to shift the container. Here are a few examples.

- If people are not focused on the task or seem to be lacking attention, the leader needs to increase constraints. This could include formulating stronger visions or goals, meeting agendas with measurable outcomes, revisiting performance objectives, or talking about what is missing during a staff meeting.

- If new ideas are not surfacing, the group has become too constrained, and the leader might form cross-functional teams to change the interactions, brainstorm possible solutions, or break into pairs to generate ideas from everyone.

- If meetings are not productive, the space or the agenda might be too constrained. Change leaders might respond by moving the physical location of the meeting to somewhere larger or with a different look and feel and/or increase the amount of time allotted for the meeting.

- The chart in Your Work at the end of this section can be used to list other ideas that might shift containers.

Difference Interventions

Differences provide the potential for change. For a system to be able to respond appropriately to the emergence in the Self-Organizing Zone, it has to allow for differences such as: approaches, beliefs, attitudes, ways of learning, or mental models based on history. Without these rich contrasts, the system can slip into "sameness" or "group think" and miss opportunities to adapt and be flexible.

When working with differences as a change dimension, leaders can pick a significant variable to watch which provides focus, or they can look at the difference the variable creates over time. For example, in a group of new people, they can watch for leadership skills to emerge, affinities to form, or ways people differentiate themselves. On the other hand, leaders can choose one variable--such as leadership skills--and observe how they grow over time in that one variable.

To diagnose the differences change leaders might consider these questions.

- In this situation, what is important to the organization? What is important to the people inside the organization?

- What differences do I see that make a difference or are important in this system?

- What do these important differences tell me about the system itself or the agents in the system?

- In what ways are the differences over constrained? Under constrained?

- Given the challenge I face, do I want to surface more difference (amplify) or reduce the amount of difference (damp)?

  ‣ Amplify example: How can I encourage dialogue around our differences so that we are able to test assertions, understand what is blocking us or create a more clear focus? This decreases constraint.

  ‣ Damp example: How can I focus on one crucial difference while ignoring the others? This will increase constraint.

The following actions describe ways change leaders can shift differences.

- If the differences in the group are too constrained, not all voices are being heard. Ask specific questions of those who are not speaking to draw them into the conversation.

- If a group is not progressing in its work because they can't settle into a decision, it may be that there are too many choices or options. Constrain their assignment by being more specific in the specifications of what they are to accomplish or limit the time available to make a decision.

- Examine job roles or descriptions to determine if these are minimizing strengths that individuals can offer the system.

- Observe dynamics in meetings to see who is influencing the group and how. A different dynamic can be created by shifting how the agenda or conversation is conducted.

- The chart in Your Work at the end of this section can be used to list other ideas that might shift containers.

Exchange Interventions

Exchanges are the ways a system connects to itself or its environment to share time, energy, information, and other resources. Unless connections are built across significant differences, no change will occur. Examples of exchanges include training, seeking input on new ideas, goals and objectives, feedback, rules, regulations and money.

Over-constraint in the exchanges can lead to isolation for parts of the system, information being tightly held, and "controls" that are too tight. Under-constraint of exchanges can lead to issues such as too much talk or gossip, miscommunication, lack of coherence across the system and lack of focus on important issues.

To diagnose exchanges, change leaders consider a number of questions.

- Is the challenge I am facing a result of exchanges?

- What is the cycle time of the exchange? (short or long?)

- What media carry exchanges in this system?

- Are exchanges one-way?

- What are the constraints in exchanges? Do they carry too much information? Too little meaningful information?

- How are people sharing information or resources?

- What information or resources are shared?

- Are resources or information transferred in a timely fashion?

- What is the impact I notice as a result of these exchanges?

- What exchanges need to exist to bring about a different outcome?

Change leaders make any number of decisions about how to shift the exchanges in a system. The following lists a few brief examples.

- Deepen the conversation (increase the constraints) by putting people in smaller groups to discuss an issue.

- Find ways to bring additional voices into the discussion (decrease the constraints). They can be from outside the system (such as the customer), or engage the quiet voices currently within the system.

- Repeat messages that are important and find ways to align conversations with the overarching objective (increase constraints).

- Make the rules consistent across the organization (increase constraints).

- Use simple rules to help people know how to make decisions when the policies and procedures don't show a clear path (increase the constraints for clarity).

- Use the chart in the Reflection at the end of this section to list other ideas that you have for shifting the exchanges.

Other CDE Interventions

Many interventions shift dynamics by influencing the conditions that are relevant in the system. These interventions work when they shift the significant conditions in the most adaptive direction, and they fail when they shift less significant conditions and/or shift the conditions away from adaptive patterns.

Table 4.2 (on the next page) presents a summary of common interventions and how they are most likely to affect change. This list is not intended to be definitive, but suggestive. Change leaders will find many additional activities that affect each of the conditions and should feel free to add to the lists of effective interventions from their own experience or theory base.

	Increase Constraint	Decrease Constraint
C O N T A I N E R	Clarify goals and mission Reduce number of people Move to smaller space Shorten meetings Tighten agenda Define projects/project management Clarify roles and responsibilities Rewrite job descriptions	Brainstorm new options Include more stakeholders Move to larger space Lengthen meetings Use large-scale interventions Engage in scenario building Encourage cross-functional teams Encourage different work venues, such as telecommuting
D I F F E R E N C E	Focus on similarities Set a dress code standard Standardize operating procedures Institute balanced scorecard Enforce standards Reduce turnover	Focus on significant differences Relax standards Encourage creativity Train on global and cultural sensitivity Tell personal stories Use Appreciative Inquiry approaches Implement training on a new topic
E X C H A N G E	Build communication templates Use standard communications Have periodic communication Increase two-way communication Clarify norms Institute specifically targeted rewards and recognitions (i.e. sales goals) Simplify/enforce performance appraisals Change sequence of talk (round-robin, talking stick) Give and receive constructive feedback Measure outcomes and process Evaluate meeting effectiveness	Increase options for interaction (break-out groups) Focus on informal exchanges Encourage social interaction Enliven commons areas Open on-line conversations Ask authentic, challenging questions Perform environmental scans Introduce dialogue practices Observe in silence Encourage personal reflections Open access to information Encourage pro and con discussion in meetings Conduct Town Hall meetings

Table 4.2

Example

Situation

As the CEO of a credit card company, George, entered his new position, he believed the company was not consistent in its change implementation. He had reviewed data from across the system and results were variable from one unit to another. George believed he needed to clarify the vision, establish more coherent expectations and communications and bring his unit leaders into a closer relationship with him and the organization's overall strategies. He began by working with his senior executive team.

Opportunity/Action

The CEO reviewed the Eoyang CDE Model with senior members of his team and explained how this intervention process would collect data and devise recommendations for review and support by leaders. Together they conducted interviews across the organization, using CDE-based questions, and identified recommendations that would support the vision and encourage self-organizing within the business unit. Their questions were:

- How would you describe the organization? Business unit? Business strategy now? How would you describe the longer-term view or the vision? (Container question)

- Who are our competitors or suitable benchmarks in our industry? What is our primary source of advantage over our competitors? What would make us the industry leader in the future? (Container question)

- What needs to happen in areas that are more vulnerable to communicate the vision more clearly? (Container question)

- On a scale of 1 – 10, how would you rate your business unit against this picture of the future? What factors that went into your rating? (Difference question)

- Where is your business unit solid? Vulnerable? What business relationships do you need to intentionally cultivate to grow and meet the future vision? (Difference question)

- What data do we collect to measure our success and progress? (Exchange question)

- What rules or norms informally govern behavior here? (Exchange question)

Results

The interview data yielded a set of 7 recommendations: 2 in the container arena, 3 in the difference arena and 2 in the exchange arena. The group, upon reviewing the recommendations, chose to take on the most challenging in the differences arena, as it had the potential to pull all business units toward the organizational vision and further galvanize the self-organizing capacity across the organization.

When to Use or Not Use This Building Block

There really is not a time when this tool does not help individuals "see" into or understand their systems. The following are some examples of specific ways to use this building block.

- In the Organized Zone, the Eoyang CDE can help leaders find ways to invigorate and rejuvenate the organization by decreasing constraints in the C, the D, or the E.

- In the Self-Organizing Zone, the Eoyang CDE can be used to help shift the conditions toward greater adaptability by shifting the C, D, or E appropriately.

- In the Unorganized Zone, the Eoyang CDE will help leaders find ways to organize the random unpredictability that exists due to the level of constraint, helping to influence the conditions that will lead to self-organization.

Tips and Traps

- When using a CDE analysis to design an intervention, it is easy to come up with a number of ways to intervene. Just pick the simplest one first and try it and see how it works. There is no secret or special way to know what to do...just do it, and then watch for results.

- When the CDE analysis reveals that a particular challenge is focused in one of the conditions, try an intervention in a different area. For example, if the difficulty emerges as an exchange problem, try a difference intervention or try shifting the container. Sometimes individuals will resist change that seems to be "attacking" or in judgment of what exists, and going to a different condition may alleviate that resistance. Additionally, a sub-set of a system can establish patterns to sustain itself, in spite of the overall needs of the system. These patterns set up a self-perpetuating effect in the system that make specific conditions difficult to shift. By moving to another condition, you can probably by-pass the resistance.

- Identify the containers that you wish to observe, influence, or change then identify the differences and exchanges within that single, identified container. Thinking of two containers at once will make it appear more complicated than it has to be.

- Because your issues may be massively entangled across levels in the organization, what appears as a difference at one level will be a container at another level. For example, if you are looking at all the people in the organization as the container, then a difference that could make a difference would be "experience." However, if you are looking at all the experienced people in the organization, then experience becomes the container, and "degree or level of expertise" could become a difference that matters.

- When you shift one condition, the resultant change will likely be fast, so be ready to move.

- When you shift one condition, it will impact all the others, so you don't have to do all three at once. You can change one condition and then observe how the others adjust. Because these changes happen quickly, the cycle time is short, and the next attempt to shift one of the conditions can be based on the results of the last shift.

- If the sticky issue is occurring at one place in the organization, try an intervention either at the level above or below. For example, if a team is interacting in unhealthy ways, look at what management is asking of the team, how management is interacting, and/or how the individuals are functioning in getting their jobs done.

- A caveat: There is a tendency to use exchange interventions first because we know them best, but other conditions may be more effectively shifted.

1. Think about your sticky issue and identify the C's, D's, and E's that are creating the patterns involved.

2. Use the chart to identify the most important C's, D's, and E's creating your sticky issue. If you run out of room, create your own chart. Important: Start by identifying one container and then listing differences and exchanges existing in that container. Once you have brainstormed all you can, identify another container, and identify those differences and exchanges. Remember that there can be multiple differences and exchanges within one container, and you will want to brainstorm several so that you can identify the most significant ones.

Container	Differences	Exchanges

Figure 4.3

3. Begin to think about interventions that would shift any conditions you are listing. Remember that you only have to shift one condition in a pattern because shifting one will cause the others to shift as well. Try one implementation and see how it affects the system. Collect data, see where you are and begin again.

Chapter 5

What Informs Action When Regulations Don't Fit?

Complicated and coherent behavior across the system emerges from simple rules.

The goal of self-organization in a system is to move toward greater fit with the environment. The system seeks coherence to optimize its adaptation and functioning, and the result inside the system is crucial to optimal functioning. A coherent system will exhibit the following characteristics.

- Reduced internal tension

- Shared goals and meaning

- Repeated patterns

- Complementary functions

- Conserved energy

- Internal and external adaptation

Coherence refers to fit and speaks to the free interplay of the agents in the system. It does not speak to the degree of certainty or agreement. It does speak to the appropriateness of the constraints in the system. For example, if a function requires high levels of constraint (Organized Zone) to operate appropriately and those constraints are not present, to increase appropriate constraints will increase the coherence in the system. As the constraints are increased and the space becomes more organized, internal tension will be reduced, agents know what they need to do, patterns of the work will be repeated as is necessary to the function, less system energy will be required to accomplish the work, and the system will be able to shift more appropriately when needed.

At the same time, a different function in the system may need operate further from certainty and agreement, as described in the Self-Organizing Zone (fewer constraints) to perform most effectively. As the activity gains the appropriate constraints, the agents will experience coherence--even in the sometimes messy environment of the Self-Organizing Zone.

Coherence in the Unorganized Zone means that agents in the system are only slightly constrained by organizational expectations, so that they do not experience the tension, lack of clarity, redundancy, or spent energy that would prevent them from functioning most effectively in the randomness that occurs when the system is far from agreement and far from certainty.

The work of the change leader is to assure that the constraints are appropriate to support the system to move toward coherence across all three Zones. If rules and regulations are too constraining, how can the members of the system assure that their decisions are aligned such that they are moving toward coherence? If expectations and relationships are not clear, how can the system have the degree of internal and external coherence that assures fit?

This building block provides the level of constraint necessary for effective decision making when rules and regulations would be too constraining. Simple rules provide less constraint that established specifications and procedures in the Organized Zone, yet they provide more constraint than normally exists in the unpredictable and random Unorganized Zone. They are broad expectations that are generalizable across a number of situations and applications, but still specific enough to have common meaning to all agents.

A short list of simple rules provides a set of guidelines for decision making individuals can use, regardless of the nature of their work. When everyone uses the same rules, decisions across the system will be more coherent, allowing all parts of the system to accomplish complementary work. Sticky issues are often the result of unspoken simple rules that prevent coherence in decision making and problem solving across the system.

Introduction

In a complex adaptive system, as long as your work is close to certainty and close to agreement most decisions and actions--both strategic and operational--can be codified into policies and procedures for the organization. While there are some tasks and jobs in the Self-Organizing Zone that can be specifically codified, it is too difficult to codify all of the relationships, interactions, questions, decisions and judgments that must be made in the system as it self-organizes.

In the Self-Organizing Zone, patterns of interaction and relationship are emergent and responsive to the environment. If you cannot rely on the "tried and true" rules and regulations of the Organized Space, how do the agents in the system know how to behave? How do they know what decisions will work? How do they meet their accountabilities when they run into challenges that don't fit in the existing procedures? Answer: simple rules.

Simple rules establish patterns of interaction and decision-making that govern individual and group behavior toward coherence of the system. The simple rules are generally unspoken, and they influence the organization in ways that are not recognized by its members.

Examples in nature include the "rules" that guide the behaviors of birds as they flock and African termites as they build their towers of mud and sand. Examples in human systems include the unspoken expectations that parents have for their children in areas of behavior and achievement. Examples in organizational systems include the unwritten rules for success that open doors for some and close doors for others.

This building block helps leaders view (retrospectively) what simple rules are currently operating, and formulate (prospectively) the simple rules that will guide future interactions and decision making.

Description

The concept of simple rules was developed from the use of computer simulation in response to understanding how to re-create system

61

activities and responses to stimuli. These programs have been used to study phenomena in complex systems such as shifts in population growth, community development patterns, nest-building behavior of termites and flocking behavior of birds.

In these simulation programs, each individual pixel of light across the computer screen is set with a short list of rules that tell the light when to turn on or off. This short list is the same for each pixel. Initial conditions are established for the program, and it is allowed to run its course, with each pixel lighting up or going dark as indicated by the simple rules. As the pixels repeat their programmed responses, patterns of light play themselves out across the screen. It is from these generated patterns that scientists are able to explore natural phenomena to look for answers to some of their questions.

Because simple rules in these computer simulations guide behavior and create patterns in the whole, they have been applied as a metaphor for human behavior. What would happen if individuals in a group agreed--either implicitly or explicitly--to observe a common set of simple, geralizable rules? Would that create recognizable, characteristic system-wide patterns of behavior, interaction and performance?

As people began to think about simple rules in human systems, they realized simple rules exist in many human interactions. Sometimes

Pattern	Possible Simple Rule
Highly competitive; "cut-throat" practices	Win at all costs
Tolerance of many diverse ideas and people	Reward diversity
Open to creativity and change	Innovate
Customer orientation	Delight customers

Table 5.1

those simple rules are explicit, as in the Judeo-Christian Ten Commandments. Sometimes simple rules are implicit, emerging from the needs of humans as they interact with each other. On September 11, 2001, in the wake of the terrorist attacks, individuals who studied the human reactions came to believe that many lives were saved because the individuals who worked in the Towers knew the simple rules about moving quickly in large crowds. They are the same rules that govern foot traffic all over that city--slower traffic moves to the right, keep moving, avoid running into others and do not let the traffic get bunched up.

Simple rules are one way to encourage coherent action in an organization and establish visible patterns of behavior. Examples of patterns that might emerge in organizations are listed in Table 5.1.

Purpose

The purpose of this building block is to:

- Provide a portable, meaningful way to understand and influence patterns that have emerged from existing interactions,

- Create and influence new patterns to bring about a desired behavioral outcome across the system, and

- Provide guidance for decisions when situations are less than predictable to assure decisions align with organizational direction.

Simple rules make up the "code" that informs people how to act. As individuals interact according to these rules, patterns of behavior emerge, forming the culture that permeates the organization. When a new person joins a group or a team, they can generally learn fairly quickly what the unspoken expectations are. Once individuals have been in the system longer, they are able to use the simple rules to guide their actions without approval by others or the instructions of set regulations.

Based on the group's beliefs and values, simple rules inform behavior in specific and operational ways. They make the beliefs and values actionable without codifying every decision or action that might emerge in day-to-day operations.

If an organization has a belief that people are of inherent worth and contributions of individuals are valued, a simple rule articulating that value can inform individual and organizational behavior. "Honor the expertise and contributions of individuals," is a simple rule that might emerge from that belief. When an employee knows he is to honor the expertise and contributions of individuals, he can:

- Make choices about staff development for himself and others,

- Respond to customer needs in a myriad of ways,

- Supervise individuals in supportive and appreciative ways,

- Provide feedback to those above and below him in the organization chart in ways that are helpful and productive.

Using the concept of simple rules, a change leader can understand the foundational elements of the culture as it exists, communicate organizational values in actionable ways, and establish organizational expectations for performance and behavior in such a way that they are "portable" and can be shared throughout the organization and across differences.

Simple rules are different from norms, ground rules and values statements, as spelled out in Table 5.2.

Simple Rules	Norms and Ground Rules	Values Statements
can generalize to fit most situations	behavioral expectations for specific times, places, or situations	state what is important, but not actionable--they don't tell us how to behave
actionable-- tell us how to behave within the organization or situation		represent commonly held beliefs

Table 5.2

Applications

Understanding how simple rules shape the current culture is the first step in applying this building block. In any organization, regardless of the culture, talking with a handful of people about what gets noticed and rewarded provides a sense of how simple rules created the culture. From the answers to general questions asked across the organization, change leaders are able to discern the existing simple rules. When these rules are unspoken, people may not understand the dynamics of their interactions, causing uncertainty and distrust.

To begin a conversation about simple rules, questions are key to identifying what people value, and they can provide a few critical ideas about the existing and desired simple rules. Such questions might include:

- What do we pay attention to?
- What is really important to us as a team?
- What would an outsider say the rules are?

- What would the receptionist say the rules are?

- How do we want to operate with each other around here?

- How do we want to treat our co-workers and our community or customers?

General Guidelines about Simple Rules

There are a few "rules" to remember about developing simple rules:

- **The rules should be designed to amplify and reward desired behavior across the organization.**

- **The rules should be kept to "minimum specifications."** The statements should be brief and powerful, outlining broad expectations, rather than attempting to specify every action and interaction.

- **Simple rules should be both generalizable and scalable.** If simple rules are generalizable, they will be applicable across the organization. The rules should also be scalable, meaning they apply to the CEO as well as the line workers. An effective test to see if a simple rule will work is to apply it to the work of any individual in the organization. If a rule applies only in one or two places or situations in the organization, then it is an instruction, not a simple rule.

- **The list should be short.** There should be seven to nine rules as a maximum. The fewer named, still capturing the intent of the organization, the better they are. At the other end, there should be a minimum of three simple rules. There needs to be at least one rule that focuses on each of the conditions for self-organizing, the container, differences and exchanges.

A short list is important for a couple of reasons. Humans cannot remember more than approximately seven items in a list, and if the simple rules are to guide individual behaviors, they need to be easily remembered and shared. Additionally, reducing the list to such a small number forces groups to clarify what are "instructions" and what the real "simple rules" are.

- **Each rule should begin with an action verb and be stated in the positive.** Most values statements are passive descriptions of what is important, leaving a gap between knowing and doing. Action-oriented statements, like simple rules, describe how to live the values. People in the organization have a more specific understanding about what is expected, rather than what is not desired.

Specific Steps for Developing Simple Rules for the First Time

Select a group of individuals who are in the best position to talk candidly and represent a cross-section of the organization.

1. Talk about simple rules and how they give rise to emergent patterns of interaction and relationship in the organization. Ask individuals to identify the most common patterns they experience in the organization. Have them brainstorm and share with the group by going around the table. Each person takes a turn sharing until everyone's list is included.

2. Based on this list identify the simple rules that could be triggering those patterns of interaction and relationship.

3. Review the list and identify patterns the group wishes to eliminate and those they wish to maintain.

4. Ask if there are additional patterns of interaction or relationships that are important to the group and develop rules to generate those patterns.

5. Review each rule on the new/revised list and determine whether the list is complete. To ensure the list is comprehensive and manageable (between 5-9 rules) ask the questions below.

   a. Which rules are redundant?

   b. Which are subsets of others?

   c. Are any rules are missing?

   d. Are there any here describing what we are going to do anyway?

   e. Do we have at least one rule that speaks to who we are as a group? (container)

   f. Do we have at least one rule about dealing with the differences among us? (difference)

g. Do we have at least one rule about how we engage with each other? (exchange)

7. Review the list one final time to be sure that the simple rules are designed to establish the patterns the group wants to see and live with.

8. Try the simple rules for awhile and check periodically to see if they need to be revised.

Examining the Past; Shaping the Future

Simple rules can be used in two ways in an organization. Retrospectively they can help change leaders understand what currently exists, by helping to identify the origins of the current patterns in the system. This application is highly useful where negative or destructive patterns of behavior have become the norm and there is a need to shift toward more productive patterns. When used prospectively, simple rules can help to shape the culture and establish desired patterns of decision making and interaction.

Using Simple Rules Retrospectively

It is sometimes helpful to look at the organization to describe current or past dynamics. For instance, when sticky issues continue to emerge, it may be simple rules are the underlying triggers. Understanding what these simple rules are is a first step to being able to change what they are. To identify the prevalent, existing simple rules, ask questions about what people see and feel as they participate in the organization. What seems important? What are the taboos? Who talks to whom?

Once those answers are gathered, patterns of language, perceptions and experience will emerge that describe the expectations and rules of engagement in the system. Ask others about those patterns and see how people respond. If you have named a simple rule, people will identify with it quickly, and will be able to tell stories about it. By honestly examining the responses to those types of questions, your sense of the simple rules emerges.

Using Simple Rules Prospectively

Prospectively, simple rules provide guidance for "decisions" about how best to adapt to complex changes in the environment. By using a short list of rules to guide decision making and planning, an organization reaps multiple benefits.

- Individuals are better able to anticipate what other members will do, resulting in greater cohesiveness and coherence in decision making.

- Individuals are better able to anticipate and understand what supervisors are expecting in decision making, contributing to greater confidence of employees.

- There is reduced need for layers of bureaucracy attempting to codify all decisions and any possible contingencies.

- The simple rules continue across time, assuring continuity through periods of change.

- Policies and procedures developed in alignment with simple rules establish formal expectations for decision making that honor individuals' expertise and contributions.

Example

Situation and Opportunity

When the Human Systems Dynamics Institute, a non-profit group, launched in January 2003, the founder and CEO, Glenda, wanted to assure conditions were established to allow and encourage the growth of both the HSD Institute and its employees, clients, and donors.

Action

The CEO understood the power of simple rules and believed they could shape interactions inside the Institute as well as between the Institute and the greater world. Glenda, working with her staff of directors, established seven rules that would guide their work.

In the years since the HSD Institute was established, Glenda and her directors have refined the list by eliminating two of the simple rules as unnecessary for the continued growth of the Institute. One rule was added to assure an ongoing ability to generate desired patterns.

Result

Initially, Glenda and the directors of the HSD Institute used the simple rules to build performance standards for employees and Associates as well as for the Institute as an organization. This list of simple rules and accompanying performance standards serve the HSD Institute in a number of ways by providing descriptions of the expectations for performance for directors, employees and Associates as they work with and in the Institute; and by providing standards against which the HSD Institute judges its own performance.

The following is a list of the simple rules that are currently in place.

- Teach and learn in every interaction
- Reinforce strengths of self and other
- Search for the true and the useful
- Give and get value for value
- Attend to the part, the whole and the greater whole
- Engage in joyful practice

As an example, these performance standards were developed to describe the first simple rule, "Teach and learn in every interaction."

- Associates indicate that the Institute staff listen in every interaction and look for ways to learn from every situation.

- All learning experiences provide participants with multiple opportunities to share knowledge about human systems dynamics.

- Published materials are informative, high quality documents that contribute to the field of knowledge about human systems dynamics.

- Interactions are thoughtful and respectful of diverse points of view that are pertinent to the field of human systems dynamics.

- Board meetings provide multiple opportunities for board members and Institute staff to learn together and from each other.

When to Use or Not Use This Building Block

Use this tool when:

- The organization wants to examine, review and understand how a proposed change will affect its culture.

- The organization wants to conduct a "what if" analysis of its culture and determine the best method to achieve an organizational change.

- The organization is facing uncharted territory and needs simple, rather than regulated, guidance for action.

- The organization needs to understand how random behaviors will or have been reinforced to become expected behaviors.

- An organization wants to determine the factors of its culture.

Do not use this tool when:

- Individuals are unwilling or unable to be honest and open as they discuss the organization's patterns of behavior and decision making.

- Management wants a different means to control, rather than guide, behavior.

- There is little difference in the group, the voice of the outlier is silenced or the tension for homogeneity is too strong.

Tips and Traps

- Don't fall into the trap of gaining consensus before a rule is agreed on. Help the group stretch by enlarging the brainstormed list. Then begin to fold by looking for common themes and having people dialogue about which rules have meaning for them.

- If a group is having difficulty in identifying the critical patterns of behavior and interaction, the facilitator may need to ask them about specific situations or bring in other stories to analyze the patterns in those to get the group to see their own interactions more clearly.

1. Using the patterns of behavior and interaction you named for your sticky issue, identify the simple rules that might have given rise to those patterns. Look to determine which of those simple rules you might want to keep and which to eliminate.

2. Thinking about the patterns you want to create in your organization to deal with your sticky issue, what simple rules would allow/ encourage those patterns to emerge? (Remember as you work: Simple rules begin with action verbs and are general statements that can apply across your organization. As you write them, ask yourself how they would be used at different levels and in different departments. If you cannot see how one would apply across the organization, you will need to go back and rework it.)

CHAPTER 6

HOW DO I PLAN IN A CHANGING ENVIRONMENT?

A system's capacity to sustain itself depends on repeated cycles of adaptive action.

How can anyone plan in a system that is unpredictable and uncontrollable--and largely unknowable? Planning in such an environment sounds like an oxymoron, but it is not. This building block describes adaptive action planning, a different way to look at how change leaders at any level in an organization plan in a way that builds the organization's adaptive capacity.

Planning in a complex adaptive system requires a different set of skills and processes. Different from traditional cycles, planning in these systems is done in short cycles of data collection, analysis of patterns, decision making and action. Then the process begins again. This iterative nature of planning in a complex system means that it is an ongoing and pervasive activity throughout the organization.

Introduction

This building block is an iterative planning process to move an organization--or parts of that system--strategically forward. It is defined as iterative because what is learned in one cycle informs the next cycle as the planning moves forward. It enables the organization to respond and adapt to everyday external and internal forces.

Traditional long-range planning processes ask organizational leaders to predict over three to five years and develop operational and functional action plans to move from a current state toward that horizon, which they see as an outcome that can be known. Traditional planning asks organizations to identify "strategic" work in addition to keeping an eye on the daily "operational" work that keeps the business running. Traditional planning asks leaders to set a plan and establish controls for the plan to be carried out.

In a system where it is impossible to predict or control, traditional planning makes little or no sense. However, planning is a critical factor in organizational life, and it must be agile and adaptive in response to a changing environment, shifting diversity in the workforce, and other patterns that emerge over time.

Adaptive action planning provides an iterative process of seeing the patterns in the environment, planning for change, and then re-scanning the environment to see what is needed next. Adaptive action planning can be used to bring about both short-term, operational, day-to-day change and longer-term improvements. It is a process that can be used at any level of the organization at any time. It requires no large-group event, long hours behind closed doors, expert consultant, or allocation of funds. All it requires is a commitment to improvement based on data from the environment and the willingness to review progress continuously.

Description

Because change leaders are dealing with systems that are always adapting, they know that to exert control removes the flexibility needed--it constrains the system by removing the degrees of freedom. The dynamics of complex systems are highly sensitive to some changes and less sensitive or insensitive to others. Finding the points of leverage can be a "hit-or-miss" proposition. A highly sensitive system will respond to small changes, tiny fluctuations or minor disturbances. To bring about systemic strategic change, it is not always necessary to initiate massive change efforts! Planning strategically can be as simple as asking "What? So what?" "Now what?" Figure 6.1 provides an image of the cyclical nature of adaptive action planning.

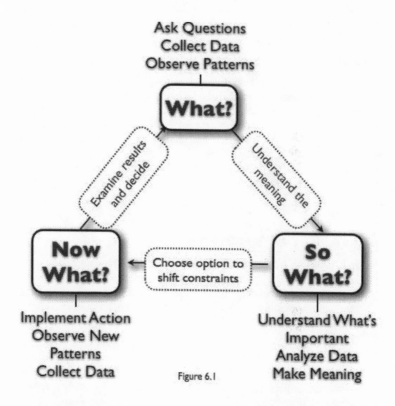

Figure 6.1

In the **"What?"** phase of adaptive action planning, the change leader works with others to collect data and information from across the system. The focus of this phase is to find out "What is happening right now?" relative to over-arching goals or strategies.

In the **"So What?"** phase, a change leader's work it to analyze the data to look at the patterns that appear to be contributing to achieving the goals and those that appear to be detrimental to departmental progress. Questions help to focus this level of analysis.

- "What are the patterns to keep?"

- "How can we shift the patterns that are not working."

- "What conditions (Eoyang CDE) exist, and how can we shift them to bring about different patterns?"

- "What is constraining us now, and are those constraints appropriate to our need?"

- "How can we establish more appropriate constraints to move toward our goal?"

As a result of this analysis, one set of actions is chosen and implemented.

In the **"Now What?"** phase, the change leader gathers further data to measure the impact of the chosen actions and determines whether or not they moved the system toward its overarching goal. If successful, the change leader returns to the data to identify a next round of actions. If the steps were not successful, the change leader returns to the data and reviews it in light of the changes just implemented and decides on a different plan of action. Both responses--to the action's success and to its lack of success--return the process back to the "What?" stage of the plan.

Why Adaptive Action Planning Works

- *It is iterative.* – The cyclical design returns to the original planning point to check progress and provide the foundation for the next step. The planning cycle is iterative as the long-term goal remains the same, feeding back into the planning as each cycle is completed—evaluating success and setting the next target.

  For instance, if a departmental leader establishes a goal of increasing productivity by a given percentage over the next year, she could use adaptive action planning to identify her first steps, based on her judgement about how best to shift existing patterns. After a period of time, she would again collect data to determine the impact of that first step, relative to the original goal, and determine her next actions. If the first step was successful, she will move to the next. If the first step was less than successful she has the option of re-designing that step before she moves on. This constant cycling back through the process moves her department through iterative cycles of planning while the overall goal remains the same.

- *It relies on patterns.* Adaptive action focuses on paying attention to and shifting the patterns of behavior and interaction that emerge in the organization. In doing so, this process addresses underlying dynamics in the system rather than surface issues.

- *It is flexible.* A cycle may take weeks or months, or it can take only days. The design cycle relates to current challenges and the solutions attempted. What is important is that most changes in the dynamics can bring about significant change in the overt activities in the system rather quickly.

- *It is multi-dimensional.* Because the parts of the organization are massively entangled, an intervention or solution tried in one part will cause some sort of shift in another part. For example, if a there is a desire to amplify a particular difference among staff members such as their individual abilities contributing to the overall outcomes of the organization--creating communications, recognizing and rewarding interdependence, mutual support and team work will contribute to that amplification and will have system-wide impact.

- *It is fast.* Working through a cycle in days or weeks, the degree of success will be known quickly because issues are attacked at their dynamic foundations, rather than at the symptom level. This foundational shift brings about change more quickly and efficiently than other forms of change.

Adaptive action planning operates within the context of a long-range direction or goal, and is specific and measurable. Using an iterative cycle of "What?" "So What?" "Now What?" helps planning moves progressively forward.

Purpose

Adaptive action planning begins with identifying over-arching goals describing desired outcomes. Through an iterative process of data collection, planning and implementation, and rechecking data, short-term action plans are carried out and move the individual toward the overall goal, as outlined in Figure 6.2 on the next page.

Setting overall goals is a simple process of saying what is desired as an outcome over time. The description only has to be enough for those who hear and use it to know the target. "We will be the best widget makers in the world." "Train every employee in the new methods." "Be the highest scoring sales person in the company." These are clearly stated, and would provide a direction for the group or individual to move.

Iterative Planning Cycles

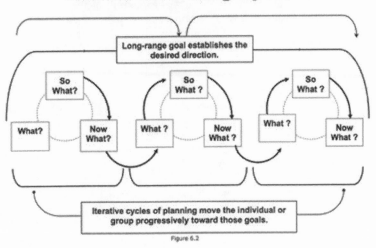

Figure 6.2

At the same time, adaptive action planning is scalable, depending on the scope of the planning. The overall goal may be one everyone agrees will take three to five years to achieve ("We will be the best widget makers in the world."), or it may be a goal that is achievable in six months (Train every employee in the new methods."), or it may take only three months ("Be the highest scoring sales person in the company over the next quarter.").

Adaptive action planning provides a simple, effective way to think about day-to-day improvements that contribute to on-going, overall effectiveness of the organization because the learning from one cycle feeds into the baseline of the next.

Applications

Adaptive action is based on reflection and learning. The unique differences in the system can be amplified because the learning cycle is short. During the cycle the individual pauses, reflects on the results, explores assumptions about what has happened and uses rich feedback loops to establish the basis for continual adaptive action.

In the adaptive action cycle, the first question is: **"What?"**

- What is the current pattern?

78

- What containers, differences or exchanges are evident?
- What is happening right now?
- What is the data?
- What do we want instead?
- What simple rules are in operation?
- Where does this challenge reside on the Landscape Diagram?
- Where does it need to reside?

These questions provide information about a decision point. Starting with the goal statement, the individual or group identifies and collects the necessary data describing the current situation--performance measures, available resources, suggested effective practices, skills and abilities of individuals on the team. This answers the question, "What?" to establish the current status of the system and identify available resources.

The second question is "**So what?**" The data is analyzed to create meaning in relationship to the overall goal.

- What containers, differences and exchanges are important here?
- Are the constraints appropriate?
- Where does this need to fall on the Landscape Diagram?
- So what does the data mean to us?
- So what more do we need to know?
- So what is the pattern we want?
- So what options are available?
- So what has to be done in the next step?
- So what can be done?
- So what must be done?
- So what steps do we need to take to change what we have now?
- So what resources will we need to take those steps?

This moves the issue to an action point of taking the necessary steps to move the question forward.

The final question, **"Now what?"** addresses actions to be implemented. Looking at this data points toward the overall target. If the steps are successful in moving forward, the next data leads to another step forward at the "So What?" in the second iteration. If the data indicates the plan was not as successful as desired, then the "What?" in the second iteration becomes a re-look at the original data and asking what needs to be done differently this time. "Now what" questions include:

- Now as we take steps, what do we see happening?

- What patterns are emerging?

- Where are we on the Landscape Diagram?

- What are the containers, differences and exchanges that we see?

- Are simple rules working to move the system toward coherence?

- Now what does the data tell us?

- Now what do we see in relation to what we wanted to see?

- Now what do we see that we were not aware of before?

- How do we shift the containers, differences, or exchanges we want to get the desired pattern?

These questions close the loop and bring you back to the 'What?" questions that start the process all over.

Example

Situation

A mid-sized school district (21,000 students) had engaged in strategic planning for approximately six years. The school board had hired a nationally known consultant to work with them to develop the strategic plan. Community members had spent hundreds of hours working with school district staff, conducting research on various topics in the plan, which consisted of eight goals, with twenty-eight measurable objectives, and over seventy action plans. None of the action plans fit into the day-to-day work of any staff members. The work was being accomplished as individual administrators had time to engage community and staff in committees to plan and implement the steps.

Opportunity

People were frustrated, and the new superintendent, Sami, who believed strongly in the value of a plan, knew that progress was not being made toward articulated goals. Her belief was they were spending a great deal of time getting ready to plan, which left little time for accomplishing significant changes in how students were served. The superintendent and her cabinet of district administrators decided to take action to simplify their planning, to align the planning process with the budget cycle, and to focus the district's work on increasing outcomes for students.

Action

As a part of the process, the superintendent and her cabinet re-visited their assumptions about planning, realizing that they could not say what would be happening in their community or schools in five years. They could, however, be more intentional about collecting data frequently and making small adjustments in their work over the next five years to maintain the movement toward high student achievement, regardless of the conditions in the environment. They also recognized that day-to-day problem solving and decision making are strategic activities and must align with the district's direction.

Rather than trying to codify all strategic work into one overwhelming set of brief action plans, they committed to approaching their daily work as they had in their strategic planning work--engaging the public, using research about best practices and why they work, measuring progress and outcomes, and seeking new and effective ways to increase student achievement.

The first action Sami and her cabinet took after their initial conversation was to articulate only one goal in the district, "All children will learn to high standards." This established the direction. They identified annual measurable outcomes as targets for the three divisions of the district--instruction, communications and public relations, and operations. Each department in the central administration and each school took on the responsibility of setting annual targets and developing plans for moving toward the district's one goal and desired outcomes. At the individual level, administrators across the district used the iterative planning process to continue moving toward their outcomes and measures.

Result

The work of the "strategic" plan became the operational work of the departments, using the adaptive action planning process. Community members continued to be involved in design phases of the planning, and they felt participation no longer was a waste of time. Schools began using central staff members to support their improvement planning and experienced real progress in the areas being addressed. Across the dis-

81

trict, strategic planning was no longer a joke or a notebook that got dusted off once a year. Planning across the district was strategic, focused and effective.

In the year after the adaptive action model was implemented, a major manufacturing company moved its headquarters out of the city where this school district was located. Not only did this shift the tax revenues for the district, it reduced the student population, which also had significant impact on the revenues received on a per-pupil basis from the state. Additionally the original, longer-range plan had called for building new school buildings in the area of the district where many of these families lived. With the loss of these students, two elementary schools opened with empty classrooms.

Within six months after that announcement, the Navy announced this city as its chosen site for operations serving military families. This announcement brought in more than enough students to replace those lost by the move of the manufacturing plant. The families that moved in, however, tended to locate at the other end of town from where the new schools had been built. The families with children moved into the area of town where the classrooms were already somewhat overcrowded. Additionally these new students were more diverse and required greater supports from the school district, due to the unique pressures that active military duty places on families.

The school district was able to respond quickly by re-setting school attendance boundaries, by re-allocating resources, and by partnering with public agencies to provide services to children and their families. This work was not easy, but it was facilitated by the fact that many community members had been engaged with the district though adaptive action planning activities, and recognized that the school district did, in fact, listen to them and respected their perspectives.

There was no way that the school district could have known that these two actions would happen, much less that they would occur in such close time proximity to each other. Nothing in their original five-year strategic plan prepared them for these occurrences. However, because their daily planning and problem solving were focused on adaptation and responsiveness, they were able to shift their focus as needed and develop appropriate services, support, and adequate classroom space for these new students.

When to Use or Not Use This Building Block

- This process can and should be used throughout an organization, with all staff applying these principles to their work, both in planning and for problem solving in today's environment.

- This process can be a part of the accountability/reward systems to assure it is embedded in expectations across the board.

- This iterative process works at all levels of the organization and in all situations of planning and problem solving.

- This building block can be used on a daily basis to assess current situation, determine viable options for action and implement actions steps toward goals.

- This building block can be used to assess patterns, determine viable actions for influencing patterns and implementing short action cycles to move continuously toward desired outcomes.

- This tool is not useful when people in the organization are not totally committed to accountability and the use of data.

Tips and Traps

- Iterative planning is only as effective as the data people collect to understand their environments and measure their progress.

- When used across the organization, planning in this way makes it difficult to hide any areas not performing. When each department states goals and results there is no way to avoid accountability.

- When a system plans in short, iterative cycles to adapt to changes in the environment, individuals require greater degrees of freedom in decision making and problem solving, shifting authority and accountability.

- Iterative planning requires vigilance in responding to the environment. Each cycle of planning requires data collection and analysis, calling for a constant flow of information that helps the organization respond and adapt. Organizations must open their boundaries and connect to their communities in different ways.

1. Use the insights from earlier work on your sticky issue to begin planning. Identify and collect other information you need to fully answer the "What?" question. One suggestion might be to think about the patterns you see and collect data around the containers, differences, and exchanges.

2. Review the data and information collected and begin working on the "So What?" question to grasp fully the impact of the current situation. Begin to think about what you want to do to change it.

3. Identify one "Now What?" action to take and develop a plan for implementing action across the system to shift the conditions holding your sticky issue in place?

4. Watch what happens and see what differences your actions make, and what you can learn from each cycle. If you are moving toward the outcome you want, start at the beginning with different pattern you want to shift. If your system is not making the changes you want, go back and collect further data about your sticky issue and start again.

Influencing Patterns For Change:

A Human Systems Dynamics
Primer for Leaders

Notes and Reflections

Notes and Reflections

Notes and Reflections

Notes and Reflections

Readings in Human Systems Dynamics, Chaos, and Complexity

 -

Axelrod, R., & Cohen, M. D. (1999). Harnessing complexity: Organizational implications of a scientific frontier. New York: The Free Press.

Dooley, K. (1996). Complex Adaptive Systems: A nominal definition [WWW document]. URL: http://www.eas.asu.edu/~kdooley/casopdef.html

Dooley, K. (2002). Organizational complexity. In M. Warner (Ed.), International encyclopedia of business and management (5013-5022). London: Thompson Learning. Available online: http://www.eas.asu.edu/~kdooley/papers/iebm.PDF

Eoyang, G. H. (1996). A brief introduction to complexity in organizations. [WWW document]. URL: http://www.chaos-limited.com/A%20Brief%20Introductio n%20to%20Complexity%20in%20Organizations.pdf

Eoyang, G. H. (2001). Conditions for self-organizing in human systems. [Unpublished dissertation]. URL: http://www.winternet.com/~eoyang/dissertation.pdf

Eoyang, G. H. (2004). The practitioner's landscape. E:CO [Online], 6(1-2), 55-60. URL: http://emergence.org/ECO_site/ECO_Archive/Issue_6_1-2/Eoyang.pdf

Eoyang, G., & Weisberg, A. (1998). Creative chaos. [WWW document]. URL: http://www.hsdinstitute.org/e-Clarity/asp_freeform_0001/ user_documents//MMAC.pdf

Eoyang, G. (2003) Comparison Between Traditional Strategic Planning and Adaptive Action Planning, URL http://www.hsdinstitute.org/learn-more/library/articles/Pre view-of_Traditional_strategic_planning_vs_Adaptive_Ac tion_Planning--handout_.pdf

Goldstein, J., Allen, P., & Snowden, D. (2004). Editor's introduction. E:CO [Online], 6(1-2), v-vii. URL: http://www.emergence.org/ECO_site/ECO_Archive/Issue _6_1-2/Editorial.pdf

(R1, A041115)

Holladay, R. (2005). Simple Rules: Organizational DNA. *Organization Development Practitioner*. Vol. 37, NO4. URL: http://www.hsdinstitute.org/learn-more/library/articles/SimpleRules.handout.pdf

Olson, E. & Eoyang, G (2001). Facilitating organization change: Lessons from complexity science. Jossey-Bass/Pfeiffer.

Stacey, R. (1996). Complexity and creativity in organizations. San Francisco: Berrett-Koehler Publishers.

Zimmerman, B., Lindberg, C., & Plsek, P. (2002). A complexity science primer: What is complexity science and why should I learn about it? [WWW document].
URL: http://www.plexusinstitute.org/services/E-Library/show.cfm?id=150

Additional resources can be found at: http://www.hsdinstitute.org

Influencing Patterns For Change:
A Human Systems Dynamics
Primer for Leaders

TABLES AND FIGURES

Influencing Patterns For Change:

*A Human Systems Dynamics
Primer for Leaders*

Glossary

These are not intended to be scientific, textbook definitions. They are, rather, working definitions relative to their uses in our book. For more complete, specific definitions, see a dictionary or thesaurus.

Agents	The actors in the system; agents carry out the work of the system
Agreement	Refers to the degree to which people involved agree on the actions to take, or the degree to which processes and procedures are mutually supportive.
Adaptive/ Adaptable	The ability of a system to respond to challenges or changes in its internal and external environments to increase its chances of survival
Adaptive Action Planning	Process of planning that is cyclical and iterative in nature; characterized by three steps: "What?" "So What?" "Now What?"
Adaptive Capacity	Skills, knowledge, and understandings that enable a system to adapt to the changes and challenges in its internal and external environments
Building Blocks	Individual concepts that contribute to a solid foundation form which to use the principles of Human Systems Dynamics. Each building block is made up of concepts, models, and applications of those models to aid in understanding and application.
Certainty	refers to the degree with which people can be sure about what is going to happen or the degree to which processes and procedures are clear enough to ensure that something will happen according to design.

Change Leaders	Anyone in a system who takes the reins of formal or informal leadership tin their own areas and use the principles of HSD to bring about change
Codify	To make into formal rules, laws, regulations or policy
Coherence	Self-similarity across the system that has the following impacts on the system itself: reduced internal tension, shared goals, shared meaning, repeated patterns, complementary functions, conserved energy. and internal and external adaptation
Complex Adaptive System	Collection of semi-autonomous agents that interact in interdependent ways such that they generate system-wide patterns; those patterns, in turn reinforce behaviors in the system
Complexity Science	Emergent branch of science that explores the non-linear nature of the physical world
Constraints	Limitations that emerge from within a system to decrease the degrees of freedom of the agents
Container	One of the conditions that influences the speed, path, or direction of the process of self-organization; bounds the system until patterns can form
Differences	One of the conditions that influences the speed, path or direction of the process of self-organization; the potential for change in a system; refers to either the multiple variables that may exist across the system or it can refer to the variance along one variable
Emergent	The process of coming into being of a higher level of structure, pattern and dynamic; it cannot be controlled or predicted, does not just happen by itself; arises out of a complex set of causes that cannot be analyzed simply as the sum of it parts
Eoyang CDE	Identified by Glenda Eoyang 2001, this refers to the combination of three conditions that influence the speed, path, and direction of self-organization

Exchanges	One of the conditions that influences the speed, path, or direction of the process of self-organization; exchanges are the ways in which the system connects to itself or its environment to share information and other resources
Fit/Fitness	Ability of a system to adapt to and sustain itself in its local environment
Generalizable	Ability of a concept or idea to be applied across different areas of thought or application
Generative	patterns that build on each other, transforming with each iteration toward fitness in the environment
Human Systems Dynamics	Emergent field of study and practice based in complexity science that explores how humans live, work and play together
Iterative Planning	process whereby what is learned in one cycle of planning informs the next cycle of planning
Landscape Diagram	Graphic based on the work of Ralph Stacey and modified by Glenda Eoyang that reflects relative shifting of constraints across a system, based on the dimensions of certainty and agreement
Massively Entangled	State of being interdependent and interactive to the degree that cause and effect cannot be clearly distinguished
Patterns	Similarities, relationships and differences that have meaning across space and time
Scalable	Self-similarity between scales of a system; or ability of a concept or idea to be applied in self-similar ways across the levels or scales of a system
Scale	Levels of organization in a system from part to whole to greater whole
Self-Organization	Process of pattern generation as a result of the interaction of agents in a system
Semi-Autonomous	Description of agents that are bound by a system, yet retain some level of choice within that context

Sustainable	Ability of a system to survive in its local environment
System Dynamics	Forces that produce change or motion within a system